HOW
TO FIT
ALL OF
ANCIENT
GREECE
IN AN
ELEVATOR

HOW
TO FIT
ALL OF
ANCIENT
GREECE
IN AN
ELEVATOR

THEODORE
PAPAKOSTAS

WILLIAM
COLLINS

William Collins
An imprint of HarperCollins*Publishers*
1 London Bridge Street
London SE1 9GF

WilliamCollinsBooks.com

HarperCollins*Publishers*
Macken House
39/40 Mayor Street Upper
Dublin 1
D01 C9W8
Ireland

First published in Great Britain in 2024 by William Collins
First published as Χωράει όλη η αρχαιότητα στο ασανσέρ in Greece in 2021 by Key Books

1

Illustrations © Thanos Tsilis

A catalogue record for this book is available from the British Library

ISBN 978-0-00-859606-4 (hardback)
ISBN 978-0-00-859607-1 (trade paperback)

Set in Arno

Printed and bound in the UK using 100% renewable electricity at CPI Group (UK) Ltd

Contents

Prologue

AN ELEVATOR does not fit all of ancient Greece, but the imagination certainly does.

Whereas archaeology as a discipline is the relatively new product of modernity, the human need to imagine the past is timeless, innate. That said, the nineteenth-century norms of scholarship that shaped archaeology also steeped it in a staid and stultifying formalism – something akin to philology, but outside, in the open air.

Let us not forget what came next: pedantry, obfuscation, treasure-hunting, and the primordial national narratives of so many: the Greeks, the Egyptians, the Chinese, the Thais, the Turks, the Mexicans . . . The nation, every nation, began to rely on archaeology for evidence of both the timelessness of its origins and the glories of its history. All this at a time when popular culture began to enter the fray and globalise the archaeophilic dream and corrupt its hierophants. As the twentieth century drew to a close, as Indiana Jones quietly ran into Lara Croft, we in Greece were in the process of confronting our own 'Vergina syndrome', overwhelmed by the diversity of an archaeological reality that is still, paradoxically, very much alive.

With this book, Theodore Papakostas helps us practise something that we have not dared to do until now. A trained archaeologist with enviable professional accomplishments, he melds the discipline with the sensibilities and approaches of pop culture. He does not shy away from playfully and light-heartedly probing the past and the role that we allow it to play in our lives. And he invites us to join him in this subversion by upending longstanding scholarly 'isms' and pieties.

A captivating storyteller who is also known by the virtual persona of Archaeostoryteller, the author returns to the archaeology of schools and university departments with consummate knowledge and a curious and open mind. He explains, he teaches, without ever losing his humorous touch. In so doing, he reveals archaeology's living range and diversity – both in Greece and in the rest of the world – not only to the non-specialist reader but also to the 'experts'.

Archaeostoryteller's antiquity may not fit in an elevator, but it certainly fits into the imagination and, importantly, the heart.

Professor Dimitris Plantzos,
National and Kapodistrian University of Athens

Author's Note

Time is a child at play
The kingdom of this world belongs to a child
HERACLITUS

THIS BOOK SERVES a dual purpose: it introduces Greek antiquity to the general public, quickly, simply, and enjoyably, without demanding specialised knowledge, and it answers common questions about archaeology, a discipline that, despite being integral to our daily lives, remains a complete mystery to many. This book came about as the result of a social media project titled Archaeostoryteller that aimed at a broader communication of disciplinary knowledge. As a popularised approach to archaeology, the book takes us on a journey through Greek antiquity, from the hidden depths of prehistory to the era that is generally accepted as bringing an end to the ancient world. And it does this by eschewing the scholarly jargon and terminology that might discourage the non-specialist reader. By the end of the book, the reader will be acquainted with the basic characteristics of all the major periods of Greek antiquity, a full picture that will allow them to locate and understand any new piece of information within this broader story or frame.

Each chapter focuses on a different ancient period, while each intervening FAQ section answers a common question concerning archaeology and its practices. The questions were selected from discussions with my Archaeostoryteller followers on social media. It is true that the classification of the periods of antiquity can be quite complicated and present a bewildering range of choices. In the book, I chose to focus on the most commonly and widely accepted periods that coincidentally led to twelve separate chapters – just like the twelve Olympians of the Greek Pantheon of gods. The book title poses a question: can all of ancient Greece fit in an elevator? I will let the reader decide. For me, it was certainly a challenge to make it all fit within the pages of this book. It was also challenging deciding on what to leave out and what to include. In the end, though, no matter whether we're talking about books, elevators, or what have you, the point is that I hope the essence of what I'm saying here captures the imagination, our way of thinking, so that it becomes something that remains with us always. One thing I do want to make clear, because I can already hear the inevitable questions about why I didn't include this, that, or the other, is that it is impossible to include *everything*. I say this pre-emptively and I hope you take it to heart: if you ask the same question, that's the answer you'll get.

I THANK ALL my colleagues at the Archaeological Service of Kilkis, where I was employed all the while I was writing this book. In particular, I thank the director, Georgia Stratouli, my immediate supervisor, Nektarios Poulakakis, as well as Maria Farmaki, Stamatis Chatzitoulousi, and Magda Parharidou. I also thank my former colleagues at the Thessaloniki Archaeological Museum, where I was lucky enough to learn so much in my

early days as a fledgling archaeologist; the colleagues throughout Greece, from Crete, Aetolia-Acarnania, Laconia, Preveza,
Abdera, etc., who so enthusiastically supported Archaeostoryteller, including from the National Archaeological Museum
and the Ephorate of Antiquities of Piraeus and the Islands; the
professors of archaeology who did me the honour of inviting
me to their classes: Eurydice Kefalidou and Marlen Mouliou
at the National and Kapodistrian University of Athens, Alex-
andra Alexandridou and Cleopatra Kathariou at the University
of Ioannina, and Stavros Vlizos at the Ionian University. I also
thank all the other colleagues (I regret that they are too many
to name individually), both within and without the archaeological service, who shared their insights and feedback with me
and who supported me during the Archaeostoryteller project.
It's a truly wonderful feeling to have the assistance and encour-
agement of your peers. I want them all to know what a source of
inspiration they were and continue to be. I thank Vasiliki Pliat-
sika and Kostas Paschalides for friendships developed over
disagreements on social media! Thank you to Tassos Bekiaris,
who helped me with his deep and enviable knowledge of prehistory. Thank you to Styliana Galiniki and Tassoula Dimoula
for the coffees, the conversation, and the unwavering support.
Thank you to Vasilis Dimou, my companion since before the
turn of the century, when we studied together in old Albion,
and whose incisive reading of the entire book manuscript was
indispensable. I still remember sending the first version of this
book – at the time structured as a monologue – to Dimitris
Plantzos, Professor of Classical Archaeology at the National
and Kapodistrian University of Athens, whose insightful
advice changed the course of the book. 'Why don't you write
it as a dialogue?' he asked, and, of course, that's exactly what

I did. For this and all the constructive criticism dating back to Archaeostoryteller's first steps, I am deeply grateful. Now I must also, per convention, issue the caveat: all error or infelicities are entirely my own and not those of any of the generous souls who advised me. And I mean it! And, of course, thank you, mother! Thank you, aunt!

I thank the entire Athens TEDx team who believed in me before I had a clear sense of where this was all leading. As well as – patience, I'm almost done! – Ioannis, Giorgos, Willy, Dimitris, Eva, Lazaros, Eleni, Christos, Christina, Giorgos, Alexandros, Sophia, and Jerry.

In closing, I want to warmly thank my agent, Evangelia Avloniti, who believed in me from the start and has always supported me. I also want to express my admiration and gratitude to the wonderful team at Key Books and HarperCollins UK, who gave their all and believed in this book and what it stands for. And, of course, I will never forget Liana Stefani, former director of the Archaeological Museum of Thessaloniki, who departed this life so prematurely on a Christmas Eve. From 2007, when I first met her, to 2019, she was the staunchest of friends and a true exemplar of incisive scholarship and ethical conduct. When I began the project on popularizing archaeology, I published my work as Theodoros Papakostas. Liana was the one who said, 'Find a pseudonym, it'll work better.' And she was right. That's how I became Archaeostoryteller.

Introduction

THERE WE WERE, two strangers standing side-by-side in an elevator, when he suddenly glanced at me and, eyes wide, cried excitedly, 'Everything flows!'

The entire scene was rather surreal. It's not often that you hear such sentences exchanged by strangers – and least of all in an elevator.

It had all begun with a turn of events at once unexpected and completely ordinary: the elevator came to a grinding halt, and we found ourselves trapped in it.

There was no reason for panic. The elevator was large, modern, all glass; the fancy kind one finds in high-end shopping centres; the kind you walk into and your heart beats like a child's when it starts its ascent, but because you are an adult, you try to keep your cool, face set.

Through the glass walls we could see the shopping centre courtyard, the sun glinting among flowerbeds brimming with ficus and ferns, muzak pouring from loudspeakers. As I have already mentioned, I was not alone; I had company. Before me stood a fellow to whom I had not given a second thought when I stepped into the elevator. Now, he was staring at me with a calm yet also somewhat perplexed expression. After a brief exchange, we immediately telephoned for help. Then there was nothing else for it but to occupy our time with conversation. We introduced ourselves and he asked me what I did for a living.

'I'm an archaeologist.'

'An archaeologist? That's great! I wanted to be an archaeologist when I was younger; I even took a course at uni, but then decided to do something a bit more practical, you know what I mean? Sadly, I don't remember anything about the classics, a little about Pericles, Socrates, the Olympian gods. Ah, I still remember that phrase that was popular among the ancients . . . Oh, what was it?' Hand on forehead, he racked his brain. 'Everything flows!' he cried with a smile of satisfaction.

'Strictly speaking, it wasn't something that was "said" or shared publicly in the ancient world. It's an aphorism of Heraclitus's, the ancient philosopher. What's more, that's not exactly what he said, but rather it's how Plato decided to sum up Heraclitus's philosophy. At any rate, as a maxim, it's both clever and concise.'

He stared at me with the expression of someone trying to puzzle out the degree of my nerdiness. Probably deciding it wasn't worth the energy, he filled the awkward silence by saying: 'The ancients, they had a way with words, didn't they? So shrewd and insightful.'

'Well, I wouldn't say it was all insightful. It's just that many of their catchphrases have gone down in history.'

'What's your favourite?'

'Hmm . . . I don't think I have a favourite. There is one by Heraclitus, though, that has always made an impression on me.'

'The same guy who said "everything flows"?'

'Exactly. He had another aphorism that goes like this: "Ὅμηρος ἄξιος ἐκ τῶν ἀγώνων ἐκβάλλεσθαι καὶ ῥαπίζεσθαι καὶ Ἀρχίλοχος ὁμοίως."'

'Are you familiar with the saying "It's all Greek to me"? You didn't expect me to understand that, did you?'

Point taken. I translated for him. 'He's saying: "Homer deserves to be thrown out of the contests and thrashed, and Archilochus too."'

'That's it? That's a silly thing for a philosopher to say!' Nevertheless, there was a spark of curiosity in his eye.

'It wasn't silly.'

'Alright, but it's not something that I'd want to get inked on me, if you know what I mean! I thought it would be something clever, insightful.'

'It was, because he was proposing a different way of looking at the world. He was pointing to the fact that we ought not to automatically admire luminaries, famous and exalted personalities, simply because that's what we have been taught to do by our parents and grandparents.'

I suspected that this would probably bring an end to our discussion.

'So the dude was trying to say that Homer wasn't worthy of respect? Is that what you're telling me? Kind of wacky, don't you think?'

I could have let it go, but I have that bug in me that makes me unable to resist talking about my work, my discipline. Besides, when I see someone goading me, convinced of something with which I disagree, it's as if I break out in an itch that I cannot help but scratch. (I must remember to discuss this with my therapist.)

'What the . . . "dude" actually said is open to interpretation.

I'm just offering you mine. Heraclitus was of the opinion that not everything about those we worship is truly worthy of our awe and respect; that the legacy handed down to us by our ancestors, to which we blindly pay homage because that's what we've been taught to do, can be just as problematic. Most broadly, he's speaking out against an indiscriminate belief in authority. He dared to express a different point of view and take issue with the greatest poet of the Greek world, perhaps even of the entire world.'

'Okey dokey.' His brows rose sceptically. 'Plus, even though I know who Homer is, I know nothing about the other one he mentions – Archilochus.'

'Archilochus was a lyrical poet. His preferred genre was erotic poetry.'

'The schmaltzy romantic stuff?' He smirked.

'No, it wasn't sentimental. I'm talking about erotica, regular erotic poetry.'

Seeing that I now had his full attention, I continued: 'Unfortunately, none of his truly "naughty" poems survive. He was from the island of Paros.'

'What do you mean by lyrical?'

'Don't get hung up on the word "lyrical". It simply refers to verse that was accompanied by the lyre, a type of music that was not focused on the glories of the past, like Homer, who composed epics. Instead, lyric poetry addressed the daily lives of people at the time – like pop music today.'

'Ah, so he was a musician! Did you say he was from Paros, the island paradise? And the verses were erotic? So just like Bruno Mars, eh, all sex and paradise!'

'I suppose you could say that: he was the Bruno Mars of the ancient world. In any case, Archilochus provides a paradigm different from what we generally associate with the ancients. As a matter of fact, once, fearing for his life in battle, he abandoned his shield and skulked off to save himself. Not only was he unashamed of this cowardice but he wrote a poem about it.'

'You're kidding! Do we still have the poem?'

'Yes.'

'What does it say? And no more ancient Greek, please,' he added quickly, before I got any grand ideas.

'It says something more or less along these lines: "Oh, enemy, you're welcome to my shield, tossed in the bush, when I turned tail, quick-heeled! It's no skin off my nose, anyway. My life is safe, and I can buy another shield any day."'

'He dumped his shield and left? No way! "Either with it or on it", isn't that what the ancients used to say? There was nothing more shameful than being a coward!'

'It's a phrase the Spartans used, "either with it or on it" – the shield, that is; in other words, come back victorious or dead. But that was just the Spartans, not everyone. Besides, did you know that Archilochus was an extremely popular poet in antiquity despite the fact that he turned his cowardice in battle into a joke? Didn't you notice that Heraclitus puts him on par with Homer?'

'Ach, you're throwing too many names at me! It's all a big muddle. When did all these characters live? Also, answer me this: why do all you archaeologists, historians, and whoever else studies the classics always overanalyse and nitpick? Sure, it was a glorious, really important time back then – we Greeks built the Parthenon, discovered philosophy, etc. – but why should we care now? Seems like a big to-do about nothing to me.'

'Not so fast! There's nothing to be gained by rushing to cancel an entire discipline! We need archaeology, my friend.'

'Well, what for? How's it useful?' he demanded, needling me.

'OK, good question. Here's my answer. Let's say that, one fine morning, you wake up and find you've lost your memory. You don't remember anything: who your father and mother are, who your grandparents are. Most likely, you would go and see a doctor. Am I right?'

'Yes.'

'Fine. So now let's say the doctor tells you that it's all good, not to worry, he can easily put things to rights, and he presents you with two choices. The first requires that you undergo therapy to recover your lost memories, the second to deliberately accept your state of forgetfulness. All you have to do is choose. Would you choose to regain your memories of the past, or would you prefer to let them go?'

'I'd want to remember, of course!'

'Why?'

'Because, mate, it's true that the past is not always pleasant, and in an ideal world we wouldn't remember every last, dysfunctional family detail, but nevertheless, it's important to me to know the main events in my life, at least. Who are the people who gave me life, and the people who gave them life? What kind of people were they? What were our good times like? What about the times when I needed help, or offered it to someone else? I mean, knowing your past is even important for medical reasons. But that's another issue. The main point is that my past defines who I am now.'

'Exactly! Since you would choose to recover the memories that you lost that morning, I think you can understand that we all need archaeology for the very same reason: because we want to know where we came from as humans. The preservation of collective memory, however, works in completely different ways than the preservation of individual memory. This is where science and scholarship come in. They help us comprehend what led us to where we are now. They can also help us determine if there is anything we can change in time to save the planet and ourselves!'

'What business of mine is the collective past?'

'Aren't you part of a community? Do you want to live your life like a robot, just going through the motions? Or do you generally feel the need to understand the world you live in and to develop your own worldview? If you want to live like a machine, puttering mindlessly through your days – sleeping, waking, eating, going to work, over and over again like clockwork each day – I suppose that's your right. But is that enough for you? No matter what line of work you're in or what your area of expertise is, you will want to know what has come before. You can't just start blind – you'll fall flat on your face if you do. So the more you open up and extend that impulse, the more you'll see how connected you are to the rest of humanity.'

'Alright, fine. The past is the bomb. But it's also a rat's nest, and it's not like I was ever really taught it properly—'

'Listen, this "I wasn't taught it properly" has become quite the chestnut – and it's also a big, fat excuse. It's not like we're talking about quantum physics. Would it make sense to you if, as a society, we simply stopped learning once we were out of school? Education does not begin and end with our schooling! In fact, knowledge is always available if you look for it, and archaeology is really accessible, easy both to discover and understand. As an adult, have you tried to learn anything about it?'

'But why should I bother with ancient Greece and the classical past?'

'Because, although it might sound like a cliché, it is true that it was the cradle of western civilisation. Don't you think it's exciting to learn when and how our entire culture began?'

'But where would I begin? It's a rat's nest, I tell you – to me, at least. I don't even have a sense of the timeline, of when the various periods were, of Alexander the Great, Odysseus, Socrates, the Mycenaeans, the Minotaur. You've studied it – can you describe in clear and simple language what the order was?'

Clearly believing that he'd finally stumped me and that I would be replying in the negative, he smiled somewhat dismissively.

'Of course! Right away, and in simple language. But to learn about ancient Greece and the classical world, to fully appreciate it and understand it, you need to see the whole picture. We need to start with what happened before the phenomenon known as classical Greece; the events, peoples, cultures that shaped the Greek world. After all, there were prehistoric cultures and important developments during the historic period that led to the "miracle" of classical Greece. It's all one continuous line of interesting stories. I can guide you through all that, nice and easy. We have time.'

My response surprised him. He stared at me, bewildered, as if trying to figure out whether I was having him on. But I just stood there, silent and smiling.

'Cool,' he said after a brief pause. 'I'm hungry, though. If only we had a something to nibble on . . .'

After I sat myself down on the floor of the elevator and he

joined me, both of us cross-legged, I rummaged around in my satchel, dug out a bag of crisps, opened it, and placed it between us. The elevator-shaft speakers provided the musical accompaniment – rock, pop, country, and everything in between – to our conversation. When the loud crunch of the crisp he had just stuffed into his mouth ushered in the opening notes to a new song, I began to speak.

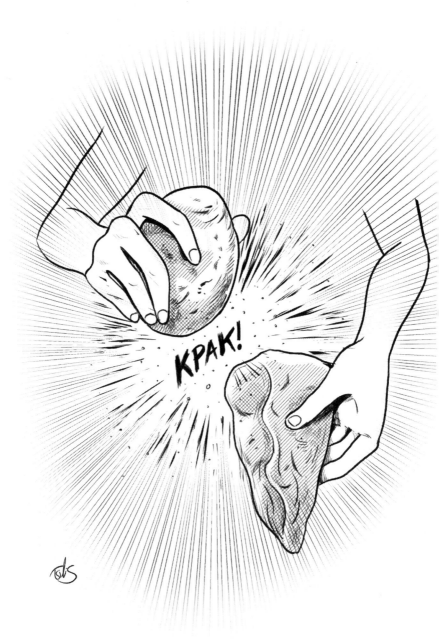

1

Like A Rolling Stone
(The Stone Age)

'ALRIGHT THEN, let's start at the beginning!'

'OK.' He looked at me sceptically. 'How did it all begin?'

'With love.'

'Excuse me?'

'I'm joking. It's just that according to Greek mythology, the first being that came forth out of the darkness and chaos was Eros.'

'Really? In other words, love conquers all?' He smiled, nodding his head suggestively.

'Always. Basically, love and power rule over everything.'

'And money.'

'Money is just the way power likes to dress itself.'

'What about love? Does love have a favourite costume?'

'Love, my friend, is always naked. In any case, let's get back to archaeology. We were talking about prehistory.'

'Weren't you going to talk about ancient Greece?'

'Slow down. We'll get to classical antiquity, and many of your questions will be answered. I think it's best, though, like I said, to start by taking a stroll through the entirety of Greek antiquity, not just the classical part. Prehistory is critical – it's interesting, fascinating, illuminating, and it tells us why and how ancient Greece came to be. After all, prehistory is also antiquity.'

'Prehistory? Do you mean cavemen, ooga booga and all that?'

'"Ooga booga and all that"?! How exactly do you imagine prehistoric humans?'

'Well, I guess . . . kind of like brutes – a bit . . . thick, I don't know . . .'

'It's a common mistake. We believe that distance in time somehow also implies an intellectual distance. In our individualised way of seeing things, we think of history as a human life writ large, and by unwittingly locating ourselves in the adult phase of that life, we relegate earlier generations to younger and less mature phases.'

'OK, but you can't say that humans haven't developed intellectually!'

'Of course they have, massively so, and each generation continues to evolve. Prehistoric humans, however, may have started at ground zero, but they were far from stupid. They were just different. Had prehistoric humans been stupid, they would not have survived. Have you any idea how difficult it is to hunt enormous wild tetrapods in order to feed yourself?'

'Like mammoths, you mean?'

'Among others. Why, you think it's easy to catch wild buffalo?'

'I've never tried, so I don't know. The only thing I've ever hunted are the chickens in the village when I was little.'

'Yeah, I'd point out that there's a tiny difference between the two types of fauna we're talking about.'

'True . . . and to tell you the truth, I never managed to

catch a single chicken when I was a boy. How *did* they hunt wild animals?'

'By using the most powerful weapon there is: the human mind! For example, we know from later sources that humans contrived to corral herds of wild animals along paths built specifically to lead them to precipices from which the startled animals would fall and die. Something similar could easily have taken place in the prehistoric period.'

'Genius! In the end, human nature never really changes, does it?'

'Ah, well that's a huge can of worms right there. If you were to ask me, I would say that there is no such thing as human nature when it comes to society. There is human biology, I'll give you that. We get hungry, thirsty; we need to piss; we hurt; we cry. This is all part of our biology, not our nature. Our nature is something we constructed and continue to adapt, as I will show you very shortly.'

'So how very different could prehistoric humans have been?'

'In some things not at all. In others, very much. They certainly had a different way of looking at the world. But, first off, they definitely had feelings akin to ours.'

'How can you say that with such certainty?'

'Because when we find Palaeolithic burial sites and see the care with which people were interred, we know that they were mourned, that someone was saddened by their loss. From that, we can surmise that prehistoric humans must also have felt anxiety, concern – for example, about whether a young woman's pregnancy would go well in the depths of a difficult winter. Or the anguish of waiting for those who had gone out hunting when they took too long to return . . . the breathless watching of the horizon as the group, now reduced in number, made its approach; the frantic attempts – knees weak, pulse racing, heart squeezed by fear – to discern a loved one among the silhouetted figures. On the other hand, they were people who had a very different awareness of themselves and the world immediately surrounding them.'

'What do you mean?'

'It's very simple. The world back then was nothing like the one we know. And when I say nothing, I mean nothing. There were no cities, no technology, none of the material goods with which we surround ourselves, and so their view of the world, the ways they interacted with it, were founded on completely different stimuli.'

'Oof, well, that's all a little too general and abstract for me. Besides, while I understand why I ought to know something about periods in history when stuff actually happened, I just don't get what there is to understand or relate to in prehistory.'

'But the prehistoric period is when everything began! That's when we became humans!'

'When are you talking about?'

'OK, let's go back to the beginning. We're talking about the Stone Age, which is divided into three periods: the Palaeolithic, the Mesolithic, and the Neolithic. Have you heard these terms before?'

'Yes, and it's obvious how they are sequenced, but that's about it. I also know that we're talking about a very early period. Why, though, is the Stone Age divided into three parts, and why does it come first? Is it just random? What about the names?'

'Yes. It really is that simple. Scholars split prehistory into three main categories: the Stone Age, the Bronze Age, and the Iron Age.'

'OK, I get it, but why are they named that? Why not call them something else?'

'Just because!'

'Are you pulling my leg?'

'Just a little. All joking aside, though, we had to call them something, so the consecutive periods were named after their predominant tool-making materials that archaeologists, in the early days of the discipline, retrieved from excavations. So, as I've already mentioned, the first period, that enormous stretch of time we call the Stone Age, is divided into the Palaeolithic, the Mesolithic, and the Neolithic, and each division has a number of other subdivisions.'

'Wait, wait! You're already losing me. Too much jargon. Let's go back to the beginning. To the first period.'

'The Palaeolithic: it's the period that sees the emergence of humans over almost all of the planet. Then, there are many, many millennia that intervene between the dawn of the human species and the revolution that brought about the domestication of plants and animals as well as the establishment of permanent dwellings – developments that are associated with the Neolithic period, and which occurred relatively recently in the history of the human species.'

'Wait, from the Palaeolithic we go to the Neolithic? What happened to the Mesolithic?'

'The Mesolithic is wedged between the other two, because, as I hope is clear, changes did not happen from one day to the next. Essentially, the Mesolithic is the transitional period between the Palaeolithic and the Neolithic.'

'And all this took place in Greece?'

'No! Globally. Greece is not the birthplace of the human

species. Nor is Europe. Humans originated in East Africa and from there they spread throughout the world.'

'All in the Palaeolithic era?'

'Exactly!'

'So when was Greece inhabited by humans?'

'We don't yet know when exactly. It's something we're looking into. Even though we have found archaeological evidence for the oldest species of humans in Greece. I won't confuse you with a catalogue of deep prehistory's human species, however, because, as you'd say, it's a rat's nest.'

'Human species?'

'Yes – we are *Homo sapiens sapiens*, but before us there were other species. *Homo heidelbergensis*, for example, or *Homo neanderthalensis*, also known familiarly as Neanderthals.'

'Ah, I know a number who are still alive and kicking among us!' He laughed.

'Yes, for some reason they are usually to be found behind a steering wheel! In all seriousness, though, to explain in the simplest way possible, just bear in mind the following: A long-gone ancestor created the first tool, and we called him *Homo habilis* – in other words, Handy Man. After that came the discovery of fire, and another ancestor got up on two legs and began to walk like we do today, and we called him *Homo erectus*, or Upright Man. That act of switching from all fours to walking on two set off a veritable avalanche of change. In any case, evidence exists for the fact that at some point *H. heidelbergensis*, *H. neanderthalensis*, and other species of human traversed what we now know as Greek land, which makes sense since it forms a passageway between the south and the north. We are still trying to determine when exactly the human species moved from Africa and spread throughout the rest of the world. Future research will provide more information.'

'In other words, Greeks have been living in Greece from the Palaeolithic period?'

'Whoa there! No. We can't possibly know that. What we do know is that some form of "human" appeared on what later became Greek land many hundreds of years earlier. We don't know which species exactly, and we certainly can't call them Greeks – they were, instead, inhabitants of this space. We can't even say if there was such a thing as a Greek ethnic group – or any other type of ethnic group for that matter – and, more broadly, how things like ethnic groups, states, even social organisation were understood that far back in time. We can't really talk about these things in prehistory.'

'You mean they didn't exist at all during the prehistoric period?'

'I mean that we cannot know if they did because we don't have any evidence, a text or some other form of information, to help us understand how they defined themselves. We simply cannot locate ethnic groups or nations in deep prehistory, and anyone who tells you different is lying.'

'But I saw an article on the internet that said—'

'You'll find all sorts of things on the internet,' I interrupted him. 'It doesn't mean that they're trustworthy, evidence-based, or founded on any scholarship. Attempts to identify nations during the prehistoric period are always politically motivated, and in the end they all fail miserably because there is simply no evidence for it. They have no basis in recognised scientific method. At any rate, prehistory is enormously important to the entire human trajectory on the planet, and whether prehistoric peoples were called Greeks, Malagasies, Egyptians, or Maasais is of little significance. Even though we cannot identify ethnic groups at that time, we can study the human species as a whole and the development of its civilisations.'

'OK, but I have a question. How old is this Palaeolithic period?'

'As a rule of thumb, on a global scale it begins around 3.5 million years ago. It is the period that we know the least about because it is also the most difficult to define and analyse.'

'Why?'

'It stands to reason, doesn't it? We're talking about a time before humans learned to document their thoughts and practices; before they began to leave great works behind; before they even had fixed dwellings. People back then were nomadic hunters and gatherers. Imagine, this was even before they began to cultivate their food! They ate whatever they managed to hunt or find growing on trees. It was not an easy life. In fact, for hundreds of thousands of years, humans endured lives of relentless hardship. Essentially, the only surviving relics of the period that are helpful in making some sense of Palaeolithic humans are their stone tools. The Palaeolithic period and the dawn of human civilisation began very simply. But if you think about it, it's a truly amazing moment.'

'What do you mean? What moment?'

'The moment when one of our early ancestors created the first tool and led us to where we are today. Of course, it all happened gradually – very gradually – but that one tool is where it all began. Humans at that time were not in a position to appreciate the import of his – or her – act—'

'*Her*? A woman created the first tool?'

'Well, is there any evidence that it was a man?'

'True . . .'

'For all humans, then, both men and women, that moment set them apart from the natural world that surrounded them, marking a first, infinitesimal step towards the creation of their own nature. It is arguably the most meaningful moment in our development as a species on this planet.'

'What exactly are you trying to say? Can you elaborate? Why is that moment so important?'

'Because it is the moment when, for the first time, human beings created something that was completely new. What is it that sets us apart from the rest of this planet's fauna? The fact that we possess the capacity to both create and destroy – even ourselves. The moment when humans created tools was also the moment when they began to shape the world around them. Nothing would ever be the same again, nor would the constant change this moment unleashed ever stop. For millions of years of life on this planet, flora and fauna had meekly and dutifully bowed to the supreme laws of nature. Yet the moment came when one species dared to "hack" nature, rise above it, and create its own – and it all started with a crack.'

'What crack? Do you mean the sound?'

'Yes – the sound made by someone striking two stones together, chipping away to create a blade. Those cracks have echoed through the many centuries since: the sound of the human species transgressing the laws of nature; a blade that carved a completely unprecedented path for humanity's future; the crack that announced the beginning of the human miracle. Humans left the warm climes of Africa and spread throughout the farthest reaches of the earth like grains of sugar spilled on a kitchen counter.'

'I see. So that was the beginning of humanity? Is that generally accepted fact?'

'It's my – and I imagine many others' – "interpretation" of what is ultimately more of a philosophical question about the beginnings of the human trajectory on this planet. Different interpretations offer different points of origin for human civilisation: when an infuriated ancestor decided to use words instead of stones, for example; or when early humans, for the first time, decided to honour their dead with a burial. When it comes down to it, though, these debates are purely academic and speculative. The truly important point is that humans created civilisation and thereby set themselves apart from other forms of life on the planet.'

'Cool! So humans went all over the earth . . . and then what?'

'It was, and continues to be, a thrilling journey; its only constant is change, which humans orchestrate but still fear, strangely enough. Anyone with a tiny bit of insight into the human trajectory on this planet, however, will get a good chuckle out of this obsession of ours for refusing to acknowledge the one unchanging element that defines who we are.'

'I disagree! I don't think that humans cause change, or things to change. It's just the way things are. We are hardwired that way – it's the way of nature.'

'Again with the nature, my friend? Is it in your nature to eat bread, get dressed, drive, read, live in buildings that tower over the earth, tame electricity, or use an elevator? And look, now you're even trapped in one!'

He stared at me, silent and pensive. 'You're serious, aren't you? There's no such thing as human nature?'

'Obviously there is, but it has to do with survival and biology, and we'd better accept it because our fates are inextricably linked. Just as we ought to appreciate our impact on the planet and the fact that we are tied to it and all its other beings. But we also should avoid using this reality as a pretext to mask what truly makes us tick. Our "nature" does not dictate our behaviour – in fact, it's the other way around. You shouldn't have chipped that stone, my friend, because it pulled you right out of nature. How were you to know? Who were you to ask? The lichen, the ferns? Or the mastodon that just ambled by with a jaw so fearsome that the last thing it brought to mind was a cozy tête-à-tête? At any rate, if you think about it, the human journey has been both adventurous and rather brief. Keep in mind that the earth as a planet is 4.5 billion years old, and life on earth began around 3.5 billion years ago. In light of how far we've come, it's truly dizzying to contemplate the fact that humans began to inhabit the planet only 3.5 *million* years ago! Again, think about it: how on earth were we meant to adapt to all that change? No wonder we have so many psychological problems! Fortunately, archaeology has come to the rescue.'

'Why? Are you telling me that's the aim of archaeology?'

'Partly in jest, of course – you could describe archaeology as a collective human therapy session during which we dig up the past to examine the root cause of our neuroses. After all, we are the most unstable forms of life in the solar system.'

'You're not wrong about that. Humans are freaky! And to be honest, we all need therapy. But tell me a bit more about Palaeolithic humans and the first gizmos they invented. Where did things go from there?'

'Well, they liked that first tool. It was handy, you see. So they made another and another. Enough to go around. Couldn't just have one person doing all the work, could you? And then someone else had a bright idea about how to improve it. That's how those early tools developed.'

'Why the focus on stone tools, though?'

'Because hand axes and other tools made out of stone and bone are the most common finds at Palaeolithic archaeological sites.'

'Didn't they use other materials?'

'Absolutely! They did use other materials, like wood, but, unlike stone, wood rots and cannot withstand the ravages of time. Consequently, what we get to discover of prehistoric humans, and in particular the Palaeolithic variety, are primarily the few odds and ends that managed to survive.'

'So what else did humans do in their infancy?'

'Art, my friend!' I roared, and my sudden vehemence startled him. 'Art! Whether it's a few minimalist pieces of jewellery or stunningly beautiful cave paintings, the human need for art ruled the roost before they even learned how to cultivate the earth and build homes! This is when people who love and live for – and by – art throw down the microphone and stride off, head held high.'

'The artist's mic drop moment!'

'So if you overhear one of our fine specimens of *Homo sapiens* yapping away smugly to his friends about how "he doesn't care about art" or how "he just doesn't get the point of it", bear in mind that your ancestors of hundreds of thousands of years ago, clad in animal skins and living in a manner only marginally differently from the rest of the animal life on the planet, even they, those "brutes" living in caves, felt the need to create art. Art, you see, was born alongside the human species. At a time when they had not yet mastered other very basic elements of survival, like farming and building, humans chose *first* to make art and *then* see to their shelter and their next meal – like true human beings.'

'Okey dokey. I get it, up to this point, at least. And after the Palaeolithic Age came the Mesolithic?'

'Yes. But I remind you that we were the ones to put a name to it, and it's just that: nominal. Don't let it confuse you. It's not like they all got together for a cave party, hung banners with "Happy Mesolithic Period" from corner to corner, counted down the seconds – three, two, one! – and then, arms around each other, belted out: "For auld lang syne, Palaeolithic period, for auld lang syne, we'll drink a cup of kindness yet, for the sake of auld lang syne." The transition was a very gradual one, and we define it in rather broad strokes to make some sense out of the incredible black hole of time that is prehistory.'

'Why, then, did there have to be something called the Mesolithic Period? How was it different?'

'Step by hesitant step, life began to change again. The Mesolithic is that transitional period between the Palaeolithic and the Neolithic, when things – very gradually – changed completely.'

'What was this period of change like?'

'Complete bedlam. Listen: we define the Neolithic as that period in the trajectory of the human presence on the planet when, finally, someone noticed that something generally grows on the spot where fruit or seeds have fallen to earth. Woohoo! Big step forward. Then, of course, came the light bulb moment: what if they were to bury a seed in the earth and wait to see what happens? Sure enough, before too long, ffffttt, there's the seedling with its tiny leaves and tiny stem. Look, look, it's growing! That's how humans learned how to cultivate the earth and grow what they needed to eat. In fact, not only did they learn to grow their food but to stockpile it, to harvest and store it for a time of need, for when the weather was bad and they couldn't find anything to appease their growling bellies.'

'Ah! I know how they felt!'

'To cut a long story short, this discovery arguably provided the foundation for property ownership and exchange, for farming led to another series of earthshaking light bulb moments: since we need land to fill our bellies, it might be a good idea to settle down for a while, don't you think? We can't do any farming if we're constantly wandering around like nomads.'

'In other words, everything changed during the Neolithic period?'

'Exactly! You see, then, how the many changes in Neolithic culture that completely overturned the status quo provide the best argument against anyone who resists change or adaptation to new ways of doing things. You know the type: "Oh, but that's the way we've always done things! Why change now?" In response, you can say that for hundreds of thousands of years, humans lived without fixed homes, without even cultivating the earth in order to have a little bread to eat, a little oil to make it easier to swallow. Would you prefer to return to the cave? Would that feel more familiar and comfortable?'

'I see. So the innovation of the Neolithic period was cultivation?'

'Not just cultivation. It went hand-in-hand with the domestication of animals. Light bulb: wild cattle were strong animals. Might they be helpful with ploughing the earth? (It turned out that when you gave the earth a good plough, the crops grew stronger.) Light bulb: goats produce milk to nurse their young, and it looks like often there's some left over. Might it be good to drink? Light bulb: sheep are covered in wool, a fibre much sturdier than the hair on human bodies. What about shearing the wool? And so on and so forth, until one of our ancestors, who ought to be worshipped as a god in Paris, Milan, and New York, had the bright idea to use the wool for clothing. Good ideas have no difficulty spreading. A traveller in unknown lands may have seen people dressed in brand new woollens and become envious. Returning to his settlement in a foul mood, he'd have tossed aside his animal skins in disgust.'

'Yeah, but wool is itchy.'

'That's right, it is, and it may well have made Neolithic humans scratch themselves raw until someone finally noticed the softness and fluffiness of cotton! To be completely fair and accurate, I also need to make it clear that these were not necessarily discoveries made by single individuals. The same ideas could easily have occurred, more or less simultaneously, to a range of different people in far-flung locations. At the same time, humans discovered ceramics: they took dirt, moulded it into different shapes, baked it, and boom: ceramic vessels! Which they have continued to make without interruption ever since. Did you know that ceramics are incredibly hardy? Time seems to do nothing to them, as long as they don't come to harm by human hand.'

'Really? How?'

'Ceramic vessels are essentially baked earth. If you let them be, they will stay intact until the end of time. Naturally, this is a great boon to science. Imagine: we still have access to ceramics from the time of their invention in the Neolithic period! It's a true godsend that now, after so many centuries of study and analysis, we can finally determine which one was made when and arrange them in serial order. Ceramic vessels are the most common artefacts found in archaeological excavations, and the long chain of development of the ceramic arts through the ages helps us identify the period we're looking at when we dig a new site. During the Neolithic era, then, everything changes for the human species. In the east, traces of the Neolithic way of life have been found from as early as 10,000 BCE. In Greece, the Neolithic begins around 7000 BCE and lasts for four millennia, more or less. Clearly, this is a very long period of time, and, as we've already discussed, it was not by any means static or homogeneous. We therefore decided to divide the period into subcategories: Early Neolithic, Middle Neolithic, Late Neolithic, and Final Neolithic.'

'OK, you're blowing my mind! There's no way I'm going to remember all that.'

'That's alright. There's no need to worry about the details. Just know that in that period of time, the Neolithic way of life spread throughout mainland Greece and its islands. With the discovery of farming, humans now had greater control over their own subsistence.'

'Is that why they worshipped gods like Mother Earth, for example?'

'We assume that they worshipped the Earth. Most likely they did, but don't forget that we are still in the prehistoric period, and we don't even know what they called their gods. In any case, they must have been pretty fearsome.'

'Why do you say that?'

'It stands to reason, doesn't it? Life, and survival, were extremely hard back then. It's likely that the human psyche imagined the gods as comparably hard. Besides, even growing your own food is back-breaking work. Farmers sacrifice life and limb to the meadow's frigid, pre-dawn frosts or the pasture's scorching, stone-melting sun, and in the end the earth may refuse to yield enough fruit, or there's a sudden hail, a blight, and all that work comes to naught. For entire millennia, humans would die of hunger when the earth did not provide enough sustenance. Deities responsible for such a state of affairs cannot fail to provoke awe and fear.'

'By the same token, wouldn't gods responsible for breathing life into ears of grain and the fruit on trees also be seen as compassionate?'

'That's a good point. There's no reason that the gods couldn't be both, their benevolence, or lack thereof, towards humans therefore signifying either favour or wrath.'

'Which is why humans, to keep on the gods' good side, invented rituals of faith and devotion!' he cried, pointing a finger high as if to emphasize his brilliant idea.

'A simplification, but true nonetheless. This, in a nutshell, was the Neolithic bloodless "revolution" that transpired – extremely slowly, it's true – and changed humanity forever. You realise, don't you, that if the changes we've talked about had not occurred, we wouldn't have either flour or freshly baked bread on which to slather a thick layer of Nutella for breakfast along with our milk and cereal. In fact, milk and cereal, too, are discoveries of the Neolithic period, not to mention the house in which we eat our breakfast. The Neolithic, as you can see, was one of the most important – if not *the* most important – period in human history.'

'You know what, mate, I agree: prehistory is both important and interesting, but it's still an enigma. You archaeologists still have a lot of work to do! It's all "perhaps" and "maybe" with you lot!'

'You're right about that, but prehistoric finds and sites are both rare and difficult to analyse. Just imagine how many subsequent histories are layered over them! An abandoned prehistoric settlement in Greece, for example, bears the footprints of all the peoples and cultures that came after, like the ancient Greeks, Romans, Byzantines, Venetians, and Turks. These sites saw battles, the building of new villages and cities, the ploughing of land over thousands upon thousands of years. During all that time, when antiquities came to light, they were either thrown away or destroyed out of ignorance. Thanks to the patience and persistence of today's prehistoric archaeologists, however, we continue to unearth new finds, new sites, that will help us fill in the picture.'

'Are there Neolithic archaeological sites to visit in Greece?'

'Absolutely, and many of them to boot! It's just that we don't have the critical mass of surviving buildings or the splendour of the classical archaeological sites to draw the spotlight of publicity. I would point to Sesklo and Dimini in Thessaly as indicative examples, but the best one I can think of is the cave of Franchthi in the Peloponnese. It's not the only such cave, but it's a truly stunning exemplar.'

I take out my mobile phone, google the cave, and show him some pictures. They don't seem to make much of an impression. His reaction is only to be expected: the cave is bare of stalagmites and stalactites; it's basically just a hole in the rock.

'That's it?'

'Fortunately for us, this cave had the rare privilege of being inhabited throughout the Stone Age, not only in the Palaeolithic, but also in the Mesolithic and Neolithic periods. It provides us with a unique opportunity to analyse their differences and developments. During the Palaeolithic period it was occupied by hunters and gatherers who used stone tools. In the Mesolithic, you start to notice some changes: the cave dwellers begin to consistently bury their dead; they take long journeys by sea and begin fishing on a large scale. By the Neo-lithic period, the inhabitants have grown in number and settled the area beyond the cave, where they built stone houses, culti-vated the earth, fished, and produced ceramics and beautiful clay idols. Towards the end of the Neolithic period, when the use of metals is becoming common, human society changes again – radically.'

'How long was the Neolithic period?'

'In Greece, it lasted approximately from 7000 BCE to 3000 BCE. Then, at the beginning of the third millennium BCE, we see the rise of the Aegean civilisations. This is also around the time that the Stone Age, with its three distinct periods, comes to an end, and we enter the Bronze Age.'

'That too has three periods?'

'That's right! As I was saying, the Bronze Age—'

'Hey, slow down! I know we're done with the Stone Age and its subdivisions, but before we keep going, can you explain one basic thing for me? What in God's name does archaeology actually *do*?'

FAQ

What is Archaeology?

'WHAT DO YOU, as a non-archaeologist, believe that archae-ology does?'

'It studies the past.'

'True, but it's not the only discipline that does that. There are others, the most well-known, of course, being history, its close relative. We therefore need a more exact definition for archaeology.'

'Fair enough. I would say, then, that archaeology involves the digging up of relics from the past. Is that correct?'

'Not exactly, because archaeology does not only involve excavation. For our purposes, I would offer the following attempt at a definition: archaeology is the study of the human past through its material remains.'

'You "would offer the following attempt"? Is that the best that you, an archaeologist, can do? Yet you're happy to poke holes in every definition I offer. What are you playing at? Don't you know how to define your own discipline?'

'Archaeology has been defined in many different ways, none of which have fully satisfied archaeologists. Indeed, most definitions have eventually been found to overlook certain aspects of the discipline. We also shouldn't forget the fact that archaeology has always had a bit of an inferiority complex about borrowing ideas and theories from other disciplines like sociology, philosophy, history, even geology, and, as a result, has tried adamantly to define how it is different. This inability to arrive at a generally agreed upon and fully representative definition of the discipline led David Clarke, one of its great scholars, to declare in frustration, 'Archaeology is archaeology is archaeology!' As if to say, I am what I am, deal with it. Therefore, to say that archaeology is the study of the human past through its material remains offers a compromise of sorts.'

'Fine, let's drop the definitions, then. Can you at least explain to me how the discipline evolved?'

'I'll explain with an analogy. Imagine the disciplines as customers at a trendy café. Some of them, the more established and important ones, have been frequenting the café for many years. The youthful and still quite naïve Archaeology stops by one day and lingers at the café entrance. The door opens and a bell dutifully announces the young woman's presence. The grandes dames in their expensive dresses and fanciful hats sitting around large circular tables covered in thick embroidered linen, fine porcelain cups of coffee or tea and trays of biscuits close at hand, turn their heads to catch sight of the new arrival. Archaeology takes a hesitant step forward and walks into the café of the doyenne disciplines.

'The ladies clustered around each table are connected, bound by common interests. They converse, share ideas, egg each other on. One day, Geology pulls something out of her pocket to show her friends. It's a humble but far from ordinary stone. Jagged and grooved, one end is quite round and only slightly altered, while the other is sharp, as if someone has chipped away at it to create a blade. "Look what I found," a pensive Geology says. From the table opposite, Theology huffs contemptuously: "Clearly, you have no idea what you are talking about, but fortunately I do! That's debris from the bolts of lightning that God sent to punish sinners way back when." Theology has a habit of offering explanations without fretting too much about things like evidence. The other disciplines go silent because they have no idea what the tool is, but it gets them thinking.'

My fellow elevator hostage interrupted me in surprise. 'Holy smokes! That's wild. Are you serious?'

'Absolutely. When the first stone tools of the Palaeolithic were found, the only "logical" explanation was that they were either debris left by bolts of lightning or arrowheads from the lances of angels sent to earth by God. At the time, it was inconceivable that humanity had existed on the planet for many thousands of years and that these were the first tools created by humans, let alone that the creation of these first tools was what, in turn, "shaped" humanity as we know it.'

'So what happened with that Palaeolithic tool at the café?'

'Geology was not convinced by Theology's explanation. Brow furrowed, she stuffed the stone back into her pocket. Besides, she had already noticed that there's a sheet-like quality to the earth beneath our feet; that it's like a layer cake that took thousands of years to bake. Wherever she looked, this observation was corroborated. Seated by her side, Archaeology listened carefully to learn all she could. This theory of the earth as layered had roused her curiosity. Very soon, Geology would find evidence for the fact that the tool was human-made, not to mention terribly ancient. The very first to hear the news was her new friend, Archaeology.

'Time passed, the café changed hands, and the large, round tables fell out of fashion. They were replaced by modern benches, sleek décor, state-of-the-art technologies, all of which were placed on the side of the café occupied by the hard sciences. Archaeology, that young upstart, began spending more and more time there, trying to ingratiate herself. Soon, she had befriended all the important sciences, and whenever she needed something she would go and ask them. They, for their part, took a liking to her, and when she joined their company, they would call her by an affectionate moniker, Archaeometry. Archaeology, now a constant presence at the café of the disciplines, where she was equally welcome among the sciences and humanities, decided that she fancied a bit of travel too. True, she had been born and bred on European soil, in the great civilisations of the Mediterranean, but she soon realised that the entire planet – anywhere that had been inhabited by humans, that is – was of interest to her.'

'So Greece and the classical world are not the central focus of archaeology?'

'Of course not! You could say that scholars interested in classical archaeology focus their work on the Hellenic space and, more generally, on the eastern Mediterranean, where ancient Greek civilisation spread. It's important to keep in mind, however, that archaeology is not synonymous either with ancient Greece or with antiquity as we know and define it in the western world.'

'Explain that, would you?'

'We've already talked about how archaeology thrives in areas of human habitation. Since humans, for many thousands of years now, have swarmed over the entire planet, it stands to reason that archaeology exists everywhere, from the towering walls of Great Zimbabwe in the tropical depths of Africa and the earliest pyramids of the Egyptian dunes to the commanding stone circles of the British Isles, the first urban civilisations of the Indus Valley, the Scythian hordes in the damp steppes of Russia, the great temples of the Maya in the dense tropical jungles of Mexico, the bold totems erected by pioneering Polynesians on the remotest of Pacific islands, and so on and so forth.'

'I love the way archaeology enables you to roam the world in your mind!'

'That's another wonderful definition: archaeology provides a playground for the human imagination.'

'Are all the civilisations you mentioned ancient? Did they all appear at the same time?'

'Some are earlier than others, but that's just chance. There's no point in making civilisation into a contest about who got there first. In any case, the earliest urban civilisations appear in Mesopotamia, Egypt, and the Indus Valley. In these regions, there is evidence of writing, architecture, and commemorative arts as far back as 3000 BCE.'

'Alright, but what was going on in Greece at the time?'

'At that time, Greece was transitioning from the Neolithic period to the Bronze Age.'

'Aha! So tell me about the Bronze Age.'

2

Hello to the Sun
(Cycladic Culture)

'THE BRONZE AGE begins just after 3000 BCE.'

'You mean that's when bronze was discovered?'

'No. Bronze and other metals – like gold, which was a big hit for its beauty and sheen even back then – had already been discovered. It's just that at the beginning of the discipline, when our methods were simpler, they observed an increased use of bronze at that time, or to be precise, of copper and its alloys, for bronze is a combination of copper and tin. This is why the literature refers to the Bronze Age.'

'The title isn't entirely accurate then. Why don't they change it?'

'That's a good question. It's not an easy or simple matter to change terminology on a global scale once we have become used to it. Besides, we need to have unanimity on how the period will be identified. So, in a nutshell, we gain nothing by changing a title. The essence of the matter lies elsewhere.'

'So how long did this Age of Bronze last?'

'In Greece it lasts from 3000 to 1050 BCE, a stretch of time that the discipline has divided into three periods.'

'I see. So I'm guessing that, like the Stone Age, there are the palaeo-, meso-, and neo- stages. Which means that we have the Palaeo-bronze, Meso-bronze, and Neo-bronze periods. Correct?'

'No. We use different terminology for the Bronze Age, which is divided into the early, middle, and late periods.'

'You're all off your rockers, mate!'

'You may be right, but there you have it: the early, middle, and late Bronze Age. What's more, the entire period is also divided into three geographical areas: the Cyclades, Crete, and mainland Greece.'

'Why this separation?'

'Because, as you'll soon see, these three regions experienced quite different cultural development. As we have discussed, while in other parts of the world great urban civilisations had already developed, in the Aegean we see the gradual creation of three quite distinctive cultures. The Bronze Age was a smash hit in Greece – in fact, not just with one, but three smash hits. This is the time of the great prehistoric civilisations; the first in line being the Cycladic in the Cyclades, obviously, followed by the Minoan in Crete, and then, bringing up the rear, the Mycenaean in mainland Greece.'

'Ugh, you're frying my brain!'

'Oh, come on! It's not that hard. We have three chronological periods that are part of the Bronze Age. Got it up to that point?'

'Yes.'

'Let's take the first chronological period, the Early Bronze Age, from 3000 to 1900 BCE. If you're dealing with the Cyclades, you'll call it the Early Cycladic; with Crete, you'll call it the Early Minoan; and with mainland Greece, you'll call it the Early Helladic.'

'I see. In other words, they're all occurring at the same time, but in different regions.'

'Exactly. Out of the three, the winner of the first talent show ever was the Early Cycladic because that's when Cycladic culture truly bloomed.'

'OK, so if I'm understanding correctly, Cycladic culture can also be referred to as the Early Cycladic period?'

'In a nutshell, yes, you can refer to it both ways. Cycladic culture reached its peak during the Early Cycladic period. Correspondingly, during the Middle Bronze Age, from 1900 to 1600 BCE, we have the Middle Cycladic, the Middle Minoan, and the Middle Helladic, which is when Minoan civilisation picks up the torch. Finally, we have the Late Bronze Age, from 1600 to 1100 BCE—'

'Let me guess! the Late Cycladic, the Late Minoan, and the Late Helladic or Mycenaean periods.'

'Exactly. Once again concurrent, but in different locations, and now it is mainland Greece's turn in the spotlight, with Mycenaean culture.'

'Phew! Finally! It's been like pulling teeth to get them all in sequence. Now tell me why each of these prehistoric cultures – the Cycladic, the Minoan, and the Mycenaean – are so unique and interesting.'

'OK. We begin with the Cyclades, where Cycladic culture developed.'

'Sorry, can I say something? The Cyclades . . . it's a strange name, isn't it?'

'Well, I see where you're coming from, but once you know its derivation, you'll learn to appreciate it! Zeus, you see, was king of the gods and quite the ladies' man to boot. He fell in love with Leto, the daughter of Coeus and Phoebe, who symbolised practical knowledge and divination respectively – in other words, the synthesis of two distinct types of knowledge in the universe – and he got her pregnant with twins. Hera, Zeus's wife, knowing that the boy born of this union would change the world as it was – not to mention the fact that she clearly was not all that happy about the situation – decreed that no place on earth, from the tallest mountain to the remotest cave, ought to provide shelter to Leto when the time came for the birth. Poor Leto was therefore condemned to wander from place to place, moaning and groaning with the pain of her contractions, until a tiny rock – so tiny and negligible that, lacking a fixed location, it drifted throughout the Aegean – exclaimed in pity: "Leto, I too know the disdain of the world; it's like I don't even exist! Come, give birth here, on me. I have no fear of Hera!" Leto thanked him and assured him that soon he would be covered in the glory he deserved for this courageous act of compassion. This is how the rock went from being unknown and negligible (*adelos* in Greek) to becoming Delos, a name that means to make manifest or apparent. And there, in the middle of that tiny island, holding on to a palm tree, Leto gave birth.

The goddesses rushed to swaddle the infant Apollo, who grabbed a golden sword, slashed through the cloth, rose on his two feet, and instantaneously grew to adulthood. Then, the entire Aegean was bathed in light. A herd of swans, come from the distant lands of the far north, circled seven times around the now sacred palm tree, and all the Olympians gathered to marvel at the new god of light. The tiny rock that had hosted the birth of the light of knowledge assumed its place at the centre of the Aegean, and the other islands gathered around to honour the sacred site. They formed a circle around it – *kyklos* in Greek – and that's how they became the Cyclades.'

'Wow! Mind-blowing.' He was silent for a few moments before asking: 'In other words, Delos has been a holy island since the prehistoric period?'

'No, I didn't say that, and it's not something we can know, so we have to tread carefully. The myth I just told you is a product of many centuries later, of the classical Greeks' inexhaustible poetic imagination. We don't know if Delos was a sacred island in the prehistoric period. We don't even know if the islands were called Cyclades, or what they were called at that time. The real point of interest is what took place there in the prehistoric period.'

'Tell me, then, about what happened in the Aegean to mark the transition from the Neolithic to the Bronze Age that resulted in the Cyclades becoming a centre of civilisation?'

'It doesn't appear to have been anything grand or earth-shaking, an invasion or a major upheaval. There was just a steady and uneventful evolution to the culture in the region.'

'Why, then, is Cycladic culture considered the first great civilisation of Greek prehistory?'

'Well, it's something that scholars in the discipline agree on. When we see a society developing characteristics distinct-ive from the basic agropastoral state of Neolithic peoples, we know that it has advanced to a new civilisational stage. This was the case with the inhabitants of the Cyclades in the period after 3000 BCE. We know that they possessed a sophisticated sense of art that bequeathed us with beautiful Cycladic figur-ines fashioned with marble so translucent it's as if it's steeped in Apollonian light. The Aegean was an immense thoroughfare that led to new possibilities. All you needed was a seaworthy vessel and the courage to face the open waters – a little pas-sion, a little nerve, and that internal restlessness that drives you to discover new horizons. Besides, the Cyclades consist of a whole lot of prime real estate slap bang in the middle of this azure Aegean thoroughfare, which has always served as an important conduit, a pole star.'

'How does that song go? Something about shining bright like a diamond in the sky? '

'Ha! Yes, diamonds shine bright, just like Aegean marble! What's more, in this period, in the Aegean, as well as the rest of Greece, the use of metals, chiefly copper, becomes more common.'

'Why is that important?'

'Metal tools means better tools. Metal weapons means better weapons. There's a general sea-change. As a result, the islands fill with settlements of people who thrive in the hospitable environment, cultivate the earth, trade and barter, and communicate and travel constantly. A fundamental and unparalleled achievement that still continues to impress, however, are those infernal Cycladic figurines.'

'Were they the first human figurines?'

'No, clay and stone figurines had been made by humans for thousands of years before we get to Cycladic culture. Very rudimentary, small-scale clay and stone figurines of humans and animals can be dated back to the Neolithic period. It's beautiful, isn't it, that humans so far back in our history tried to capture these likenesses? By the time we get to Cycladic culture, however, we see the creation of a truly impressive school of art focused on human figurines – primarily female, although there are some males, and, oddly, some notable ones of musicians – in a great variety of shapes and sizes, ranging from quite small to truly enormous. This is why Cycladic culture is so important.'

'But why is this a testament to an advanced culture?'

'Because when a people attain a high level of artistic accomplishment it means that they have advanced beyond the rudimentary stage of simple subsistence and that they are now using their minds in new and extended capacities; that they are now occupied with loftier pursuits and aims, so to speak.'

'Well, those figurines are truly beautiful! I like how they're so white, and kind of abstract.'

'Oh, but they weren't white! In fact, they were decorated in bright colours, which faded or completely wore away with time.'

'So then how do we know that they were coloured to begin with?'

'Through special testing of the traces of ancient pigments that remain on the surfaces of the statues. Remember the field of archaeometry that I mentioned earlier? That's the kind of thing it does. Now, of course, we've become accustomed to the whiteness and minimalism of the figurines and that's what we admire most about them, but don't forget that they became desirable objects in the contemporary period, when they influenced modern art and also, sadly, have been the cause of dozens of disastrous illicit excavations, all for the purpose of selling them on the black market to collectors around the world.'

'Ugh! What a catastrophe!'

'Yes, both an immeasurable and, most importantly, irremediable catastrophe. The majority of Cycladic figurines in museums around the world today are of unknown provenance and lack all all the relevant information that derives from a proper and scientifically documented excavation. You can imagine what a disaster for the discipline this lack of basic information about the figurines' use and meaning is. We'd have access to this information if we knew where and how they were found.'

'It sounds like not an awful lot is known about Cycladic culture.'

'That's true, we still don't know all that much. We do know that people lived in small settlements; that they had a sophisticated sense of art evident in their popular culture, from the figurines that we talked about to various surviving, very beautiful vessels fashioned out of either clay or marble. We also know a bit more about their burial customs.'

'Why is that?'

'It's generally "easier" to find undisturbed cemeteries, which are, after all, built underground. Settlements, on the other hand, were built for the living and were lost more easily, when the living passed on. Overall, the type of research we do is no easy feat. Most of the islands are rocky and their terrain not easily accessible for the few and limited teams of archaeologists. Moreover, relics from such a distant past, which are rare to begin with, are also, to a great extent, damaged by the many intervening centuries. No matter what, though, we plug on with the research.'

'You think it's likely that we'll learn more in the future?'

'Yes. That's the only thing I'm certain of. We've even made some new discoveries in the past couple of decades. Archaeology, as you know, is both a surprising and unpredictable discipline, and in the twenty-first century it held a great surprise in store for us concerning prehistoric Cycladic culture of the third millennium BCE. There is an island called Keros in the Aegean, south of the island of Naxos and next to Koufonisi, that has been uninhabited for many centuries. On that island, antiquities smugglers found large quantities of Cycladic figurines that were dispatched to collections around the world. The curious thing is that these figurines were invariably broken. Initially, we thought that the smugglers, driven by self-interest, broke them on purpose to sell more pieces.'

'But that initial theory was wrong?'

'Excavations on the island revealed that the smugglers were not to blame for the breakage; that, in fact, the figurines had been broken since the prehistoric period. As if this were not enough, the volume of broken marble figurines found on Keros was astounding. So much so that the number of figurines from tiny little Keros exceeds those from all the other Cycladic islands combined! It became clear that Cycladic people would travel to Keros from the surrounding islands with the intention of breaking the marble figurines that they had taken such trouble to carve with their own hands.'

'That's crazy!'

'Wait, because it gets even crazier. Right next to Keros, there's a tiny pyramid-shaped islet called Daskalio, which, in prehistoric times, used to be a promontory of Keros. Excavations revealed that Daskalio's pyramidical shape was enhanced by thousands of tons of white Cycladic marble brought from elsewhere to cover the island and build the terraces and structures that glittered in the azure light. The highest peak on the island was most likely its holiest spot, if not the entire Aegean's.'

'A prehistoric Delos?'

'Ha! I like the way you're thinking. We cannot prove it, not yet at least, but it's a great idea. Keros and Daskalio were clearly of great importance, and hopefully in the future we'll come to fully understand why that is. Let's continue with our story, though. At some point, the small Aegean islands were overshadowed by a stirring giant. Crete, the largest island in the Aegean, clambered up on stage and grabbed the mic out of the Cyclades's hands. "Take a seat, Cyclades!" Crete crowed. "I'm gonna show you what it means to be born a star!"'

'You're talking about Minoan Crete?'

'Yes.'

'Aha! I remember that it was discovered by someone called Evans.'

'Arthur Evans made it a household name, yes.'

'Was Evans the "first archaeologist"?'

'Of course not! What are you talking about?'

'Well, I thought . . . perhaps . . . Who was the "first" archaeologist, then?'

I sighed. It was time to explain some more of my discipline's history.

FAQ

Who Was the First Archaeologist?

'THE FACT IS, there is no such thing as a "first archaeologist", because the evolution of the discipline was gradual. Initially, it appeared as a form of antiquarianism: in other words, people who were interested in the past, just like the antiquarians of today. Among them, however, certain individuals took some crucial initiatives that set archaeology on the path to becoming a real discipline.'

'Like? Give me some names.'

'Let's go to Ancona, a small city in medieval Italy, at around 1400 CE, to the house of a merchant family, whose son, Cyriacus, is the apple of their eye. Cyriacus de' Pizzicolli was a rather curious bird. He fell madly in love with antiquity and abandoned hearth and home to roam the world, searching for ancient relics in the dense darkness of the Middle Ages, a period when this pursuit couldn't have been further from people's minds. He also became known as Cyriacus of Ancona, a city that was actually named by Greek settlers from Syracuse.'

'Does the name mean something?'

'Yes, it comes from the word for elbow, *ankón*, because the promontory that protected the ships in the harbour was shaped like an elbow.'

'So it's accurate to say that Cyriacus put some "elbow grease" into getting archaeology off to a good start!' He smiled smugly, and I smiled back.

'Anyway...Cyriacus noticed various relics in his neighbourhood and the broader vicinity, all just lying there nonchalantly in the sun, completely ignored by everyone else, and was consumed by the desire to know what they were and what they told us about the past. This internal itch grew and grew, and he was on pins and needles to discover more antiquities. He left his country and wandered the entire Mediterranean, exploring, observing, and keeping detailed notes about it all in his diaries. He ended up writing six volumes! Many archaeological sites and monuments were located and identified for the first time by Cyriacus. He sowed the seed. His gift to us was the countless notes and sketches he left behind. Many of the antiquities he identified have since been destroyed, but thanks to Cyriacus we have a sense of what they were like. Some have called him the father of archaeology.'

'OK...so there's no official "first archaeologist"...does that mean we also don't have a first archaeological site?'

'No, that does exist!' He hadn't expected that, and was taken aback. 'The first official archaeological site was established many years later, entirely by accident. I'm referring to the cities built on the foothills of Mount Vesuvius near Naples, in the region of Campania in Italy, the most important of which were ancient Heraklion, now known as Herculaneum, and Pompeii. You probably know the story. Small, sleepy provincial towns, with their shops, their wealthy mansions, their baths, their taverns, their amphitheatres and meeting houses. Until one day, in 79 CE, the volcano Vesuvius convulsed with a violent sneeze, and all those people, both rich and poor, who exchanged "good day"s and quarrelled and struggled so hard to stand out from the crowd, died together, en masse, in a matter of hours, covered in a thick layer of ash that preserves them intact through the centuries. Until we get to the eighteenth century, when a flower-seller who grows his wares in the environs of the villages now located on top of those ancient cities, gets his three sons to dig their well deeper because it has run dry. The more they dig, the more antiquities they unearth: statues and ancient treasure galore! The local aristocracy gets wind of it. Keep in mind that this is taking place during the Renaissance, when people are beginning to broaden their minds and value education, so the relics are much admired. People begin to become curious about the past.'

'Just a sec, mate . . . I've seen archaeologists dig things up using only a tiny little brush. It's a painstaking process! Do they use that method to dig up entire cities? Did they know how to dig carefully and systematically like that back then?'

'No. They dug blindly and quite crudely. They had not yet developed the professional standards and methodology that we use today.'

'When did archaeologists begin using that methodology?'

'Good question. It didn't take long. A case in point comes a tiny bit later, at the end of the eighteenth century, from some-where very far from Italy: the newly constituted United States of America. It was Thomas Jefferson – the third president of the USA – who led one of the first truly professional excavations.'

'What? Are you kidding? Did they even have classical antiquities in the Americas?'

'No, of course not, but didn't we say that archaeology is one thing and classical antiquity another? Archaeology has a role to play wherever humans once lived.'

'Yes, but weren't we talking about Greek antiquity?'

'We were, but because now we are talking about the his-tory of the discipline, we're taking a brief detour to give you a sense of how the discipline as a whole evolved on a global scale. Don't worry, we will return to ancient Greece shortly. Listen – Jefferson owned land that contained burial mounds, in other words, man-made mounds built over prosperous graves. Until then, the Europeans who had travelled to Amer-ica full of dreams and delusions of superiority could not even conceive of the fact that the local populations of Native Ameri-can Indians they encountered had once built such complicated tombs. They therefore attributed their creation to an unknown and sophisticated people who had disappeared before the arrival of the Native Americans. Jefferson was the first who dared utter a big, booming, empirical, 'Hmmm, maybe not. Let's look into this . . .' He began excavating those tombs on his land, and he unearthed at least a thousand graves containing relics that shed important light on indigenous culture. In this instance, he did not let racism blind him.'

'A big bravo to Thomas!'

'Yes, his contribution was not only to the discipline but to our general humanity. At around the same time, there was a

German lad who went by the name of Johann Joachim Winckel-mann—'

'What a name! How do you remember all that?'

'True, it doesn't have much of a showbiz ring to it. In any case, the lad was a restless soul and he travelled to Italy, where he visited the newly compiled collections of recently retrieved ancient statues. Winckelmann fell madly in love with ancient art of both the Greek and Roman varieties. Diving into the discipline head first, he developed the foundations for the study of classical art. He too has been called the father of archaeology, or of classical archaeology at least.'

'What about prehistory? Is the poor thing an orphan?'

'Not at all! A Dane made a number of important discoveries through his excavations in the northern regions of Europe. He was called Christian Jürgensen Thomsen.'

'Ah, another great name for the marquee! What did he do?'

'In the cold, damp climate of northern Europe, Thomsen had neither dazzling statues and ancient temples to excavate nor detailed written sources to help him explore his country's past. He gritted his teeth and resolved to create the founda-tions for the study of the most distant and unknown reaches of the human past. After all, historical documents are all well and good, but what do we do when we don't have any? Do we simply throw in the towel? Thomsen's torch was the first to shed light on the deep darkness of prehistory, providing the stimulus for the discovery of the human past. He was the one who divided prehistory into three separate periods: the Stone Age, the Bronze Age, and the Iron age. He too was called—'

'Let me guess: the father of archaeology.'

'Exactly. Then along came a Frenchman, Jacques Boucher de Crèvecoeur de Perthes—'

'Wow! The names are just incredible. Couldn't they come up with something a little catchier, like Cher, Sting, Bono, Gaga?'

'May I continue?'

'Yes.' He pursed his lips and looked me in the eye.

'This Frenchman discovered human skeletons, stone tools, and, remarkably, elephant and hippopotamus bones in northern Europe. These two animals, of course, had vanished from the region for millennia, and this prompted him to wonder: "How could this be? Perhaps humanity existed and travelled the continent much earlier than we thought . . ."

Not surprisingly, the spate of questions this conjecture unleashed shook the biblical narrative to its very core. Jacques was never called father, but without a doubt his insights were enormously influential.'

'Well, that's a relief! Your discipline has more fathers than is good for it!'

'Well, there's no point in losing sleep over the question of individual paternity. The entire notion is meaningless because it took a group effort to build the discipline's foundations.'

'Why are we only talking about fathers, then? Weren't there any mothers involved?'

'The truth is that archaeology as a discipline is the product of a male-centred world. Later, when women claimed their rightful place after immense effort, there were many important women who distinguished themselves on a global scale. In Greece, for example, the first woman to direct her own excavation in Crete before the First World War was an American called Harriet Boyd Hawes.'

'Was she the first woman archaeologist?'

'No! Not even close! She was simply the first to direct her

own excavation in Greece. Until then, the prevailing sexism of the time had relegated women to the library and the academic side of the discipline – naturally, almost always in complete invisibility. At a stretch, they might serve as assistants to the excavation, albeit still cloaked in obscurity. There is no more blatant example than that of Mary Ross Ellingson, who, again just before the First World War, worked on the excavation of ancient Olynthus, a classical city in the region of Chalkidiki in northern Greece, where she examined an enormous amount of material. Her research, however, was published with no acknowledgement by the male archaeologist – who also happened to be her mentor – who was credited with the discovery of the site! It wasn't until much later, in 2014 in fact, that the truth came out. Thankfully, however, sexism in the discipline has been eliminated to a large extent.'

'Not completely?'

'Archaeology is just like the rest of society, my friend. Sexism is by no means entirely dead; it is manifold and manifests in subtle ways beyond the obvious. But let's not go down that path, because a little while ago you said that you wanted me to explain Greek antiquity to you, and we aren't even done yet with prehistory.'

'Oh, yes. Where were we?'

'Minoan Crete.'

3

Get into the Groove
(Minoan Civilisation)

I CLENCHED MY HAND as if holding a microphone. 'Ladies and gentlemen, your attention please. It is now time for the main act, the grande dame of Greek prehistory, in around 2000 BCE. It's her turn to take the stage and steal the show. Minoan Crete was the Madonna of Greek prehistory. Like the Madonna song, she was a masterpiece, and a real success to boot. She even dropped the Phaistos Disc, at the top of the charts for thousands of years. We have a small problem with the lyrics because we can't read them yet, but let's hope that at some point we'll solve that mystery. In any case, if you're wondering why that disc became such a success, one thing I can tell you is that it never went platinum. It's still as small and round a piece of clay as when it was found abandoned in a corner of one of the basements of the Palace of Phaistos. The hieroglyphs impressed on it have not yet been deciphered.'

'Why do you say that? I've read somewhere that someone was able to read the disc.'

'Not true.'

'How can you be so sure? What if they're right? In your opinion, then, what do you believe the Phaistos Disc says?'

'I'm not going to tell you what I believe because there's no point in that. I will tell you, however, why what I or anyone else believes as an individual is completely meaningless. In short, theories in and of themselves do not suffice. They need to come with proof. Yet the symbols found on the Phaistos Disc have not been found anywhere else, and the sample is too small for us to come to reliable conclusions. In other words, we cannot cross-check a researcher's proposed interpretation with other samples to see if it, in fact, applies. If we ever find other tablets with the same symbols, we may have some hope of finally deciphering it. Until then, whoever wants to can come out and declare their opinion – they have every right to do so! But if that opinion cannot be substantiated in a way that convinces the majority of the scholarly community, then it is just that: an opinion that is not admissible by the discipline.'

'Why, though? Why shouldn't these opinions, as you call them, count for anything?'

'Because this is how the humanities and social sciences work. There are always people who have divergent opinions and interpretations about certain matters or texts. This is why scholars are duty-bound to publish the results of their research: to allow other specialists to examine them, and if they prove to be convincing and accepted by the majority, then all is well and good! If someone baldly asserts that they have managed to "read" the Phaistos Disc, however, then we are dealing with unsubstantiated opinion, pure and simple. Besides, the truly impressive point is that the disc is "printed". In other words, every symbol has been made with a hieroglyphic seal that was pressed into the soft clay as many times as needed. Which is exactly how, many years later, the original letterpress was designed to work.'

'Why has the scholarly community not accepted any of the interpretations of the disc up until now?'

'Because we have no other scripts like the one on the Phaistos Disc to verify these presumptive interpretations. The disc is very small, and all presumptive interpretations are, at once, equally plausible and equally unsubstantiated.'

'So what else is ancient Crete famous for besides this Phaistos Disc?'

'Crete's rich soil allowed all forms of cultivation to flourish. This, in turn, was the foundation for a very healthy self-sufficiency. Moreover, the Minoans had already mastered the seas, and their vessels regularly criss-crossed the eastern Mediterranean.'

'Fishing boats, you mean?'

'No, my friend! A regular fleet. We're essentially talking about a "Minoan rule" of the Aegean Sea. They also caught a glimpse of developments in the east: their palaces, their great civilisations, their cultural and artistic achievements. We don't know what the Minoans called themselves, but we do know that the Egyptians called them *Keftiu*.'

'They came into contact, despite the distance?'

'Naturally, and most likely in quite a large variety of situations. Exchange of goods? Trade? Engagements and marriages? Anything is possible.'

'OK, what's this about engagements? You didn't just say that out of the blue!'

'No, you're right, I didn't . . .' I grinned. 'I will tell you all about it shortly, and it will blow your mind, because I'm certain you would never have suspected it. Let's not get ahead of ourselves, though. Minoan Crete, as I was saying, saw what was happening in the rest of the world, and this inspired her to do the same, but in her own inimitable Mediterranean style, with charm, elegance, and an indisputable love of nature and good food. Crete was the great diva of antiquity. The Minoans built palaces – what am I saying? – mega-multiplexes of palaces! At around 2000 BCE, during what we call the Protopalatial period, the first clusters of royal palaces were built in Knossos, Phaistos, Malia, and Zakros. Some three hundred years later, in the Neopalatial period, these same palaces were rebuilt, even bigger and grander.'

'Why did Knossos become more renowned than the others?'

'Knossos, among the earliest and largest of the various Minoan palaces, was unparalleled in size, extravagance, and magnificence, not only for the duration of prehistory but for many subsequent centuries. It contained monumental staircases and central courtyards, enormous storage rooms, reception spaces, baths, paved roadways, a water management and sewer system, even a water-flushing latrine!'

'It didn't lack for anything, I see.'

'Well, it did lack something – indeed it was quite a striking lack. Something that makes Minoan civilisation even more impressive. Those almighty palaces lacked fortifications.'

'What do you mean by that?'

'The powers that be were so formidable and successful, the political and cultural systems so stable and strong, that there was neither a feeling of threat nor the need to build tall, defensive walls around the city centre. And what blooms in this type of environment of well-being and prosperity?'

'I want to say flowers . . . but you'll say I'm being a jackass again. Besides, since everything was so fine and dandy, I'm sure they were all living the good life!'

'I'm not sure that was true all the time, but they certainly had a great culture. First, they liked athletics. Inspired by the pastimes they'd observed in the east, they created their own forms, like bull-leaping and other types of acrobatics.'

'What do you mean bull-leaping?'

'It was a sport at the time. They'd get a bull charging through the square and young men or women would try to somersault over the bull's horns, onto its back, and land on the other side with as much grace and spectacle as possible. The arts also flourished rather spectacularly, producing works that ranged in size from large, imposing monuments to tiny handmade objects. In fact, some of those pieces of decorated jewellery are so small they make you wonder how the poor craftsperson didn't lose their sight! They also had those mind-bogglingly beautiful wall paintings, with colours so alive and vivid that you'd think they were painted just yesterday.'

'Yes, I remember seeing some of those wall paintings in a documentary. They're impressive.'

'They're what brings us back to that issue I was telling you about earlier – the marriages between the royal families of Knossos and the Egyptian pharaohs. Did you know that Minoan wall paintings were found in one of the Egyptian palaces, at the archaeological site of Tell el-Dab'a?'

'Real Minoan wall paintings?'

'So similar, at least, that they were either painted by Minoan artists or by artists who had consummate knowledge of Minoan art, because besides the style they also depict bull-leaping.'

'What the devil? How could that be?'

'Well, back then, royalty married royalty as a form of diplomacy. It's extremely likely, therefore, that an important royal wedding took place between an Egyptian royal and a Minoan princess.'

'And she brought her handymen with her?'

'Probably to make her new home look familiar.'

'What else did she take with her?'

'We don't know, but we can imagine. See how archaeology provides an opportunity for your imagination to explore situations that had never even occurred to you before?'

'Yes – the truth is that I had not imagined Minoans dancing on bulls in Egypt.'

'Imagine, then, that princess boarding a ship, gazing nervously at the picturesque mountains of Crete from her vantage point in the harbour, surrounded by chests packed with the personal items she is taking on her journey. A favourite dress? A childhood toy? Something, in short, to serve as an anchor and give her courage on her way to the unknown. We don't even know if she knew whom she was travelling to meet, a stranger who spoke a different language and worshipped different gods. Gods that had been described to her as enormous stone beings with animal heads, and cities, containing palaces, surrounded by giant walls, built along the banks of an enormous river that traversed endless sandy plains until the eye could see no more. A place where gigantic, strangely shaped stone monsters loomed among the dunes, their four sides meeting in a sharp angle like an arrowhead piercing the sky. These structures were allegedly so large and so old, built a thousand years before she was born, that she had difficulty believing the stories she had been told. In her world, the biggest and most magnificent thing she knew was Knossos's central square, where they gathered to watch the bull-leaping.'

'Yeah . . . when you tell it like that, there's definitely a more human dimension to ancient discoveries. I went to Knossos when I was little, but I never dreamt that they had danced and leapt over bulls during their celebrations.'

'The Minoans weren't just about entertainments, weddings, and festivals, though. They developed a writing system to keep track of their financial affairs. After all, can you imagine managing such great palaces, with complicated systems and networks, without notes? If your brain is all you've got to rely on day-in-day-out, you're going to wear it out! At first, they used hieroglyphs—'

'Egyptian writing, you mean?'

'No, Cretan hieroglyphs. We use the word hieroglyphs because they're reminiscent of the Egyptian variety. Soon, however, this writing system developed into something more complicated that we now call Linear A.'

'What kind of language was it? Do we know?'

'A writing system is one thing and language is another! A spoken language can be represented in a variety of writing systems. And no, we don't know which language Linear A represented, nor have we managed to decipher it yet. We have some sense of how it works – especially numerical symbols – but generally we have not managed to truly understand it. That's a discovery that lies in store for future generations of scholars.'

'There's a certain mystique to Minoan Crete, isn't there – a grandeur?'

'True. There's also a lot of mystery. It's not for nothing that we're still dazzled by it. The women were powerful, equals to men; they were girls who just wanna have fun, and walk in the sun, and if the fancy struck them, they'd tuck a snake under each arm and saunter around bare-breasted.'

'Yes, I've heard about the Minoan snake goddesses. Why the snakes and bare breasts?'

'Why not?'

'What kind of a response is that?'

'I'm just messing with you. The fact is, we just don't really know what Crete's snake-toting, bare-breasted women were about, nor do we truly understand Minoan religion and ideology because we lack written sources and we've already talked about how foolish and dangerous it is to mistake supposition for incontrovertible fact. Broadly speaking, however, it's evident that all these separate details are indicative of an elaborate philosophy of life and religion. This alone is impressive enough, and the source of innumerable myths. It is not accidental that, according to legend, Zeus was born on Crete.'

'In the Minoan period?'

'We don't know that. By the time we get to the Classical period, though, the entire Hellenic world acknowledged Crete as the birthplace of the father of the gods. This is how it all goes down in the myth: Zeus's father, Kronos, a rather superstitious type who always has an ear for a good prophesy, alarmed by an oracle's declaration that one of his offspring will dethrone him, comes to the supremely rational decision to devour them all whole. (To be fair, contraception had not yet been invented.) In any case, one gulp, and down the hatch and into his belly they go. After all, what is a hapless father of the gods to do? Lose his throne? God forbid! Or, more accurately, god devour. His wife, Rhea, tired of giving birth to infants that end up in her fertile husband's stomach for brunch, decides to hide Zeus, the most recent of her newborns, in a cave in Crete. When Kronos, smacking his lips, asks her where the baby is, she serves him a rock fajita instead. To hide the infant god's cries from the bottomless pit that is his irascible father, the Curetes and other local minor gods of battle go to the cave and beat their shields in feigned combat.'

'Didn't it occur to anyone that the baby might have been crying because there were a bunch of big clods beating each other up right there in front of him?'

'Ah, you're asking too much if you expect sensitivity to child psychology at that time! In any case, Zeus suckles a goat, Amalthea, and grows into a young man just bursting with ambition: he wants to conquer the world! He forces his father to vomit forth his siblings, who, despite being awash in gastric juices and rather muddle-headed from the inhospitable environment in their father's gut, quickly bounce back and stand by the young Zeus's side in the war he launches against his father and his uncles, the other Titans. Long story short, the younger generation wins and gives Zeus dominion. The new sovereign, now at the zenith of his glory, decides it's wise to take advantage of his newfound power to also conquer the female sex. He goes all the way to Phoenicia where, transformed into a bull, he steals away a young woman, Europa, and brings her to Crete for some R&R and TLC. The entire continent of Europe is named after this toothsome lover of Zeus's.'

'Well, thank God for that. Imagine if he'd fallen for an Amarantha. Today we'd be talking about the Amaranthan Union and the Amaranthan Court of Human Rights.'

'It was on that same island that Minos, the son of Zeus and Europa, reigned supreme. He was a great king, but he defied the will of the gods. One day, a bull appeared from the sea, sent by the gods. Minos was supposed to sacrifice it to them but, awed by the animal's magnificence, he refused to kill it and decided instead to keep it. As punishment, the gods made his wife,

Queen Pasiphae, fall in love with the bull. The fruit of this love affair was a half-human, half-bull child – the Minotaur. Product of a dysfunctional family, the Minotaur evidently suffered from psychological issues, probably afflicted with a complex that was not diagnosed in an effective or timely fashion, for he ended up with a penchant for eating people. The rest of that Minoan soap opera is more or less well-known. The young hunk Theseus steals onto the island, kills the Minotaur, takes Ariadne, the king's daughter, and hightails it out of there. "Ugh, those foreigners! Coming to our country and plucking the best of our blooms," hissed the Minoan gossips as they paced the backstreets of Knossos in their ornamented dresses.'

'Do you know how I imagine the Minoans? As a happy and amiable people who didn't go to war, and spent their time singing and dancing in flower-filled fields. A free and easy life, full of strong, bare-breasted women strutting their stuff. Is that how it was? An ideal, nature-loving society?'

'That's an absurd oversimplification, my friend! Minoans were buried with their weapons. If they weren't warlike, why did they have them? We should think twice before we make the Minoans into an ancient version of John Lennon and Yoko Ono. Also, don't forget that the image we have of Minoan culture is the one that Arthur Evans propagated – an image that made him famous. We now know that the Minoans weren't "flower children" by any stretch of the imagination. In fact, they even made human sacrifices.'

'Impossible!'

'Yet true! Here's a little FYI: by an incredible stroke of luck, we discovered a temple, Anemospilia on Mount Juktas, that was destroyed by an earthquake. Three skeletons were found in one of the rooms. Two of them, a man and a woman, were found to have died from the earthquake and the fire it sparked. The third skeleton, however, that of a young man, was found with legs tied, lying on an altar-like stone table, a knife beside him. We therefore think it likely that in a period of high seismic activity, people decided that the sacrifice of a young man might appease the gods. At the moment of sacrifice, an earthquake ended up burying them all instead.'

'Whoa! This really tarnishes the image we have of our ancestors. I feel like we're blackening their name.'

'Why this fixation with a flawless image of the past? It's not like we are paragons of perfection now, are we? Why, then, do we expect the past to have been perfect? Can we not be impressed by the accomplishments of past societies while also being fully cognisant of their inevitable human flaws? Those were harsh times. Would you go to a prehistoric person to complain about the lack of disability access at the temple? It would be absurd, wouldn't it?'

'Yes, I suppose it would. Can I say something unrelated? You know what I've been wondering all this time you've been talking about Crete? What was the deal in the Cycladic islands? Had their culture just disappeared?'

'Of course not! The very opposite, in fact. It's just that during that period the Cyclades obviously fell under Crete's sphere of influence.'

'What sphere of influence are you talking about? Politics? Economics? Culture?'

'In all likelihood, all of the above. If I had to pick one, I'd say culturally for sure. The island of Santorini provides us with proof because her volcano erupted at around the end of the seventheeth century BCE. This time, though, the volcano got a bit cranky first, and its moans and groans sent the locals out of there like bats out of hell, which is why we haven't found any corpses from the eruptions – at least, not yet.'

'What do you mean "not yet"? Has the entire site not been excavated?'

'Just a portion of it. In any case, after a while, the volcano literally exploded, because volcanos have anger management issues and when they get really het up their eruptions are cataclysmic. Volcanic ash blanketed the entire ancient city that lay at the location of today's village of Akrotiri. The artefacts we've dug up there reveal a truly unexpected standard of living.'

'You mean like a prehistoric Pompeii?'

'Exactly like a prehistoric Pompeii. We found streets and squares, entire neighbourhoods of well-built, two-storey houses with every imaginable comfort inside and decorated with incredible wall paintings. Don't go imagining an apartment in the bourgeois part of town, with a paltry two paintings on the walls in tastefully neutral colours – one the requisite still life, the other a seascape. These houses attested to a truly enviable standard of living, with their elegant carved furniture and beautiful vases. And all this was preserved because of the eruption of the Santorini volcano.'

'The eruption that also destroyed Minoan civilisation?'

'It didn't destroy Minoan civilisation. It's been decades since we debunked that myth. It certainly gave it a hard time, but it didn't destroy it.'

'Well, then, how did Minoan civilisation fall, if it wasn't the volcano that did it?'

'No civilisation just crumples up and disappears in a day because of one event. At some point, for reasons unknown and in a way that we can only guess at, they were invaded by mainland Greece. While Crete prospered, mainland Greece had begun to overcome its longstanding introversion. At some point, around 1600 BCE, we see the initial formation of a society with an aristocracy, an army, and a raging appetite for conquest. The Mycenaean world, which initially comprised only the southern part of the mainland, built its own palaces and soon spread in all directions. Either through trade or with its army, it ran rampant through the Aegean, Crete, and the coast of Asia Minor. Crete, with its self-indulgence and high standards of living, was a real temptation for the Mycenaean Greeks, both as object of conquest and inspiration.'

'OK, but when push comes to shove, all you archaeologists do is theorise. You offer a theory about the Phaistos Disc; you offer another tentative theory about the decline of Minoan civilisation . . . Can't you just dig, and find out what truly happened?'

'It's not so simple, my friend. Archaeology isn't just about digging stuff up.'

'What do you mean?'

FAQ

What Do You Mean By 'Not Just Digging Stuff Up'?

'ARCHAEOLOGY isn't just about digging to see what's buried in the ground. That's the function of excavation. The discipline's scholarly process begins long before we break ground and continues long after we've retrieved our artefacts. In fact, the true heart of the discipline is in determining how to interpret the finds.'

'What do you mean by "interpret"? I thought the things you find provided their own answers?'

'Are you serious? Do you truly believe that we glue our ears to a stone, a vase, or the earth and catch a few words of wisdom? Artefacts don't talk. The silence of the lambs is all we get from that lot. Besides, they have a rather fatal flaw: the tendency to agree with anything *we* say. In other words, if you put your mind to it, it's not all that difficult to get the data to support your favourite theory. This is why much more important than the objects you find under the earth is the issue of how you go about interpreting them.'

'Is it really that complicated?'

'Look, many years ago, archaeology was a simple, rather naïve discipline. You could even go so far as to call her clueless. She'd see something, interpret it in the first, most obvious way that came to mind, and then move on to the next thing. Or she'd just sit there besotted, mooning at the beautiful knick-knacks she'd found in the ground. Here's an example of her method: if a vase that looked to be ancient Greek or Celtic was found in a certain location, she'd assume that Greeks or Celts must have lived there. We'll call this type of approach culture-historical.'

'OK, fine, but I don't see anything wrong with that.'

'There's nothing right about it either. It's a methodology that's simplistic, limited, and, when all is said and done, very dangerous. The most compelling reason being that it was consistently used by various peoples as ideological justification for their imperialist practices as they laid claim to different regions, lands, and heritages. Moreover, it completely misses the essence and magical complexity of human culture as a whole.'

'But I still don't understand why, if a vase from Hellenic antiquity is found in a certain location, it doesn't necessarily mean that Greeks lived there.'

'I'll explain with an example. Let's say that sometime in the far future, someone excavates my house. Even though they'll find very few things of Greek manufacture, there will be plenty of objects of Japanese, German, Italian, Turkish, Korean, and many other provenances, despite the fact that no one from any of those countries has ever set foot in my house, let alone actually lived there. If my ethnicity were to be guessed at based on the objects in my house, then I truly am an international man of mystery. Or, if I happened to make off like a bandit at a Korean appliances sale and my house is now full of them, should that future researcher take me for a Korean? Does that make sense to you? A second example demonstrates the dangers in this way of thinking. During the rise and rule of German Nazism, archaeology functioned, on the whole, as a Pool of Siloam, providing the moral justification for the Nazis and their supporters to occupy foreign lands where ancient Germanic artefacts had been found. A case in point: Poland. We all know how that story unfolded, especially between 1939 and 1945. If you don't know, here it is in a nutshell: it did not end well. There are plenty of examples of the use of the past to bolster a contemporary ideology – Soviet archaeology, for one, almost exclusively interpreted social relations and systems through a Marxist lens; the archaeology of apartheid South Africa denied the existence of ancient indigenous cultures and deemed every excavated artefact evidence of European colonisation; closer to home, Greek politics for most of the nineteenth and twentieth centuries relied on archaeology to fan the fires of nationalist pride, and whitewash and glorify the past.'

'How do we avoid these pitfalls, then?'

'When archaeology realised that it was not enough to find antiquities, classify them, and identify their ethnic provenance; when it realised that it needed to dig deeper, so to speak, and interrogate the obvious, that's when the young discipline came of age. The process began in the 1960s, and by the 1970s it had fully come into its own. This was the time of "new archaeology". Remember how I talked about archaeology as a young woman who liked to hang out with the hard sciences? Well, during this period, she copied them and sought to identify the processes that drive cultural phenomena. This was the making of "processual archaeology". Civilisations were seen as systems supported by sub-systems, generating analyses and statistical models galore.'

'I see. So all the theoretical issues were finally resolved. Archaeology had finally found its true purpose?'

'No. Sadly, it wasn't that simple. At some point, all the statistics and hyper-analysis began to get in the way, and it became clear that this approach had its pitfalls, too, because it did not account for either the uncertainties and paradoxes of the human agent, or the fact that archaeologists themselves are afflicted with all manner of predilections and biases. That's when we see the advent of "post-processual archaeology".'

'What now is this post-processual archaeology?'

'It's an archaeological approach that seeks the human within the objects. Supposedly, post-processual archaeology was to serve as a complement to its processual counterpart, but scholarly disagreements raged back and forth.'

'You all like to make things complicated, don't you? So how did things end up? Is archaeology still in search of her identity?'

'Now, archaeology is trying to combine all the aspects I just mentioned, while never losing sight of the complex and manifold nature of human existence. From gender archaeology, which examines the meaning of gender in society, to social archaeology, which investigates the economic and social facets of antiquity, together they comprise the great puzzle that is the discipline of archaeology.'

'I don't get it, mate – why all this big to-do about the theory of archaeology?'

'Because, as we already talked about earlier, if you don't know why you are studying antiquity and what you are trying to find, if you don't have a clear sense of the parameters of what you are working on, you cannot provide clear interpretations. In which case, you are nothing more than a treasure hunter, and you won't get any answers. To get the right answers, you must ask the right questions. An example is what we were just talking about: what led to the fall of Minoan civilisation?'

'Ah, yes! That's where we left off. You were saying the Mycenaeans invaded. What was up with *that* civilisation?'

'OK, so here's what was up . . .'

4

Getting No Satisfaction
(Mycenaean Civilisation)

'SOME TIME AROUND 1600 BCE we enter the period that we call the late Bronze Age. Proto-Greek tribes, already having descended into mainland Greece and been influenced by both Cycladic and Minoan civilisations, begin gradually to develop an urban culture and build palaces.'

'So the Mycenaeans were the first Greeks?'

'The Mycenaeans were the first documented Greek-speaking culture. It first developed and spread throughout mainland Greece, before moving to the Aegean Islands, Crete, and even Asia Minor, Macedonia, and southern Italy. It was named after its most famous palace, which was located at Mycenae. Mycenaean palaces dotted the Greek landscape, and Mycenaean structures have been found as far as Macedonia and Asia Minor. The most important palaces, besides the one in Mycenae, which was also the most renowned, were located in Pylos, Thebes, Iolcos, Tiryns, and Midea. It's almost certain that there was also one on the Acropolis of Athens, which was demolished and subjected to an extreme makeover at a later date.'

'Was Mycenaean civilisation as splendid as Minoan?'

'In general, it's good practice to refrain from "comparing" civilisations. What's the point? They had many commonalities, but also great differences.'

'What was one of the great differences?'

'The Mycenaeans were much more warlike and generally enthralled with the art of war. In fact, the Greeks of the later historic periods always refer to them as formidable warriors.'

'You said they spoke Greek?'

'And they wrote in Greek! By slightly adapting the writing system they found in Crete, they developed Linear B script.'

'In other words, they adopted the Minoan language?'

'Didn't I warn you not to confuse them? Writing is one thing, and language another! Keep in mind that in our time, "Greeklish" refers to the Greek language written in the Latin alphabet.'

'I see! What do you mean, then, when you say that they wrote in Greek?'

'We have found thousands of tablets written in Linear B. The first Linear B tablets, however, were found in Crete, so at the beginning we thought it was Cretan writing, even though we had also found Linear A, a more ancient writing system, there. In the meantime, dozens of other Linear B tablets began surfacing in the Peloponnese. We now know that Linear A was the Minoan writing system and Linear B the Mycenaean. It's only in the palaces, of course, that these tablets were found. Indeed, at the Pylos palace in the Peloponnese, we found the royal archive, destroyed by the same fire that brought an end to the palace complex. As a matter of fact, it was because of this disaster that the tablets were saved.'

'What do you mean?'

'At the time, scribes used to write on unbaked clay shaped

either like a tree leaf or a page. The tablets were then classified by subject in wicker or wooden boxes, and archived. When the season ended and a new cycle of accounts, etc., began, they would take the pieces of clay – the tablets, as we call them – and use water to resoften and reuse them.'

'Ah, how sustainable of them! Recycling existed in the second millennium before Christ!'

'That's right, but to get back to my main point: because the Mycenaean palaces came to a violent end, with fire and axe, the fire that destroyed the Pylos palace baked the clay tablets and preserved them until they were found thousands of years later.'

'In other words, the Mycenaeans were literate.'

'I don't think that holds in general! Only a few people knew how to write. There were a couple of dozen palace scribes – we've been able to distinguish them by their distinctive hands – who would take pieces of unbaked clay, mould it in the palms of their hands into the shape of an olive leaf for shorter entries, or the page of a small book for longer ones, and use something sharp to record long lists of objects that went in and out of the palace.'

'Didn't you say that we've found thousands of such documents? What are they about?'

'The vast majority are accounting ledgers.'

'Ugh! What a let down.'

'Yes, but they're neither useless nor do they lack useful information.'

'I don't give a toss about accounting.'

'Fennel, celery, cumin, cardamom, mastic, coriander, sesame, pennyroyal . . .'

'What? Are you quite alright there, Mr Archaeologist?'

'I'm referring to herbs and condiments that were used by the Mycenaeans in their cooking. You jumped to conclusions about the value of the palace accounting ledgers, but, they've just shown you that in order to enjoy a good meal, with ingredients taken from the bounty of the Mediterranean earth, both you and the Mycenaeans of 3,500 years ago use the same ingredients! You see, they enjoyed good food just as much as we do.'

'Wow! OK, I'm impressed. What else do these tablets reveal, then?'

'Indirectly, an awful lot, even some of the ins-and-outs of their society. For example, there's a tablet that refers to a "judicial" dispute between the priesthood and the local authorities. Eritha, priestess to one of the deities – we don't know which one exactly – was trying to claim a huge piece of arable land, and the community authorities – *damos* in Mycenaean Greek, as opposed to the modern Greek *demos* – were dead set against giving it to her. We also know that during a ceremony – probably the enthronement of a new king called Augeias – they threw a crazy feast.'

'Some hundred kilos of meat, I bet!'

'A hundred? Think again, my friend! An entire cow, twenty-six rams, six sheep, four goats, and seven pigs. All together over two tons of meat. Not to mention the thousands of kilos of fruit and vegetables, honey and wine!'

'Augeias? There are also names on those tablets, then?'

'Not only human names, but also their animals'. We know, for example, about farmers who named their cattle things like "Spotty", "Blackie", "Blondie", "White-Face", and "Wino".'

'That's brilliant! And are there references to other important figures?'

'Yes, there are references to Carpathia, a priestess who, by the looks of it, was a real thorn in the side of the powers that be.'

'Why?'

'Because she was either lazy, or simply chose to ignore her responsibilities. One of the tablets mentions that she controlled two plots of land which were lying fallow even though her obligation was to cultivate them. My personal favourite of the tablets, however, is by a scribe who must have been bored because, at some point, either while waiting for the information he was supposed to record, or because it was just a slow day, turned the tablet around and began to draw a dancing warrior! I can't help wondering what he was thinking about. "Oh, Mother, even though I really wanted to become a warrior – or perhaps a kind of ancient Fred Astaire? – I've ended up a boring scribe in the public sector!"'

'You know what really impresses me? The fact that we were actually able to decipher the script!'

'After long and strenuous effort by researchers.'

'But why can't we read Linear A yet?'

'Because of a very important difference: we don't have the same volume of text that we have for Linear B. As I've already mentioned, you need a sufficient amount of source material to test any potential deciphering system. The second reason is that, clearly, Linear A tablets are not inscribed with a language that is familiar to us. We've made attempts at deciphering it based on the Greek language, but without success. If Linear A was a form of extremely ancient Greek, we would be able to decipher it. This was the case with Linear B, from which we've been fortunate enough to deduce so much important information about the society, its economy, and the workings of the palace complexes, including the fact that they had slaves.'

'Yeah, that doesn't surprise me.'

'We also know that there was a priesthood in possession of land holdings that were clearly separated and distinguished from public and private ones. In fact, the Greek word for sanctuary, *temenos* – an area set apart for devotion to the gods, where people made sacrifices and other offerings – derives from the verb *temno*, to cut, that we first find in the Linear B script.'

'Aha! I see that priests have had money and power since forever. Is that all? What else has Linear B taught us?'

'We've learned about the gods that were worshipped back then. No great surprise here: the pantheon of Mycenaean Greece is chock-a-block with the gods that we know from classical Greece, with some notable exceptions. We have Zeus and Hera, but also Diwia, Zeus's female counterpart, and Drimios, Zeus's son.'

'This is the first time I'm hearing about Diwia and Drimios! Who was this son of Zeus?'

'A deity, and part of a very ancient religion that did not survive into the following centuries. There are other deities of that period that will be equally new to you, like Enyalius, a predecessor of Ares; Paean; Potnia; Eileithyia; Trisheros. You will surely have heard of Athena, though, and Artemis; Hermes; Dionysus; Apollo; Poseidon – but not Posidaeia, his female counterpart.'

'Are all those names listed on the tablets as invocations?'

'Remember that these are accounting ledgers, so many of the gods are mentioned on tablets that list the offerings they received. There's a very important tablet from Pylos that mentions a ritual taking place in Sfagiana, during the month of Plowistos, when the gods received gifts and sacrifices. Potnia received a gold kylix – a cup with a shallow bowl – and a woman;

Posidaeia a gold phiale – a libation bowl – and a woman. Trisheros got only a cup . . . he must have been a D-list god, that one.'

'Hold on – you mean they were sacrificing people?'

'In all likelihood, yes. There is a small possibility that we're talking about people who were consecrated to the service of the deity as "slaves to the god", but I don't think that's very likely given that the tablet refers to a sacrifice. To interpret them as slaves to the sanctuary is, probably, our attempt to render the situation more palatable. Besides, there are references to the fact that at a celebration for Poseidon, offerings of both gifts and sacrifices were made – a gold kylix and two women – while at Zeus's sanctuary we learn that Zeus got a gold vase and a man; Hera a gold vase and a woman; while Drimios, their son, got only a vase.'

'The poor boy was robbed! Those ancestors of ours were a bloodthirsty bunch. I would never have guessed.'

'The Mycenaean period was harsh, but at the same time it was well-organised and, by the looks of it, prosperous.'

'Yeah, as long as you didn't end up a human sacrifice at one of their festivals! At least now when you go to a village festival you'll find boiled goat's meat on the menu, and not your sister-in-law on the spit.'

'The priesthood was clearly powerful. Sovereignty, however, was held by the palace, and the governance system was characterised by a pronounced and complicated hierarchy. The ruler of the region and supreme leader was the Wanax. This is why the palaces they lived in were called *anaktora* in Greek.'

'Did they not have regular kings?'

'They did! But they were much lower down the hierarchy. The second most significant person in the hierarchy after the

Wanax was the Lawagetas, or the leader of the people. He was followed by the Ekwetai and the Korete and Porokorete. Note that the word for king, *basileus*, was a title of a lower order, for a chieftain or local official. Hold on to this bit of information – you will need it later.'

'Argh! A bloated public sector has been our lot since time immemorial! What exactly did all these people do?'

'We're not yet sure of the role played by each title. Clearly, one of them was responsible for military matters, while the others focused on issues like trade, administration, and religion. It was a complex society. How else were they to build such monumental palaces and works of art?'

'I want to hear about the Lion Gate of Mycenae. I went there on an excursion, and it made an impression on me.'

'The Lion Gate, the main entrance to the splendid citadel of Mycenae, is at once pretty as a picture and rather two-fisted. The lions obviously symbolise the bravery and strength of the powers that be. Because there wouldn't have been room for the lions' heads in the limestone triangle on which they are carved, we think that they jutted out and were turned to look at those approaching the gate from below. Lord Elgin, too, visited the site and wanted to take the gate with him. He tried to find some hired hands in the surrounding villages but, at the beginning of the nineteenth century, the region of the Argolid was short on the manpower necessary to move such massive slabs of rock. Elgin left empty-handed. Of course, he did take half of the Parthenon Marbles, and the Greeks are still at loggerheads with the British over them.'

'Well, the Mycenaeans sound like a really powerful and important lot. What became of them?'

'At some point, Mycenaean civilisation went belly-up.'

'Why?'

'That's the million-dollar question! We've spent decades and decades trying to identify the causes of the fall of the Mycenaeans. Were they internal? Was it changes in climate that negatively impacted agricultural production? Social turmoil? An invasion? All of the above? Most likely, there was no one single cause. In any case, a theory has made the rounds that fleets of marauding hordes, perhaps originating in Sardinia, were ploughing through the eastern Mediterranean, laying waste to everyone, entire nations falling like dead leaves in the wake of their incursions. These raiders, a motley confederation of various unknown races and tribes, are called the Sea Peoples. The entire Mediterranean became their hunting-ground at around the end of the Bronze Age. In their rampage of sacking and plundering, they may also have attacked Mycenaean Greece, as they did all the great cities of the eastern Mediterranean – the Hittite Empire, Syria, and Palestine. They even had the nerve to lock horns with almighty Egypt, but ended up biting off more than they could chew. To be fair, Egypt only just managed to stop them. This great turmoil, and the decline of dozens of states, brings an end to the Bronze Age.'

'But, wait . . . isn't that when – oh, what's it called? – the Dorian Invasion happened?'

'Yes, that's true – some argue that Mycenaean civilisation was brought to its knees by the Dorians, another tribe of Greek people that used to live in the north. The fact is, though, that this alleged invasion is not supported by the archaeological finds. There is absolutely no evidence anywhere of a new culture that would support the theory of new influences entering southern Greece. Some have tried to argue that the geometric pottery prevailing in Greece after the fall of the Mycenaean palaces was in the style used by Dorian populations. But that is simply not the case. First, because, as we've already established, it is never a good idea to identify styles of pottery with the presence of particular ethnic groups. If that were the case, the archaeologists of the future would be correct in hypothesizing that all of us – and I mean ALL of us – belong to the ruling state of Tupperware! Second, geometric patterns began in Attica, a region which, according to what we know, the Dorians bypassed on their way to the Peloponnese and therefore never set foot in.'

'So what are you saying – that the Dorian Invasion didn't happen?'

'No, I didn't say that. But it happened in a way that likely did not send shockwaves through all of Greece, as we once believed. At the very least, it did not necessarily lead to the fall of Mycenaean civilisation.'

'Whoa! In other words, another rat's nest. You have a lot of work ahead of you.'

'That we do. But it's not a bad thing. Can you imagine how boring it would be if we had all the answers to everything? In any case, what's important, irrespective of the reason, is that the powerful system underpinning Mycenaean culture collapsed. What followed was what we call the Greek Dark Ages.'

'Dark Ages? When did all that – the collapse and then the darkness – take place?'

'At around the end of the twelfth century BCE, Mycenaean civilisation was on its way out. In the middle of the eleventh century, at around 1050 BCE, we enter the Dark Ages.'

'A question: sometimes you use terminology like "Late Helladic" or "Mycenaean" age, and other times you give me exact dates! What's the deal? Why is the chronology so ridiculously complicated? How many chronologies do you actually have?'

'OK . . . let me explain.'

FAQ

How Are Archaeological Finds Dated?

'YOUR QUESTION is not an unusual one. There are two kinds of dating methods for sites and their artefacts: the relative and the absolute. The relative refers to the chronological system that we archaeologists use to distinguish among the different periods of antiquity. It is usually based on pottery because that is the most common find. Absolute dating provides a specific year based on the world calendar.'

'I'm having some difficulty understanding . . .'

'Here's an example: let's take a particular vessel and say it is prehistoric, from the Mycenaean era. According to relative dating it is of the Late Helladic III period, while in the absolute system it is from 1400 BCE.'

'Why do we need two systems?'

'Relative dating is of more use to archaeologists and researchers, while absolute dating is the final goal, and more comprehensible to the remaining interested parties. The relative method is useful because of its flexibility. What's more, newer finds may lead to adjustments in the correlation between relative and absolute dating. The relative method is beneficial when we're still in the throes of the research process because it affords us the possibility to do our work without being tethered by absolute dates until we can make an informed decision. The backbone of relative dating is the examination of the different layers of earth at a given site and the classification of the arte-facts found.'

'What do you mean by "examination of the different layers of earth"?'

'The layers of earth at any given site correspond to differ-ent periods, and in each layer different types of artefacts will be found. Since the most common (and useful) artefact is pottery, it allows us to establish a chronological sequence of the forms and patterns that were used. That's what we call a typology.'

'Can you explain a bit more what you mean by this?'

'Here's a contemporary analogy: don't you find it fairly easy to figure out a general timeframe for different models of car belonging to a particular automobile manufacturer? You are, essentially, identifying their sequence because you are visually familiar with the gradual evolution in that manufacturer's car models over the past century. When you see a 1960s model, you will know it as a product of the 1960s, because you are familiar with the general look – its typological development, in other words. That's exactly how it works with ceramics. A similar process of typology can apply to many other finds, like statues, metal objects—'

'But not with all finds?'

'No, it's not possible with all, because some functional objects were so generic that they did not change much over the years. Ceramic objects, by a really long way, are the most common finds that actually exhibit characteristic changes over time. That's why they're so useful as benchmarks.'

'Well, then, how do you date in the absolute system?'

'Do you remember when we were talking about archae-ology as a discipline and how it became thick as thieves with the hard sciences? Well, that's one big favour that playful little

Archaeology kept asking of them: to help her date her arte-facts. All these methods, of course, have their limitations and drawbacks, but I'll explain how some of the main ones work. The best-known method for dating organic materials is called radiocarbon dating. We know that C-14, a radioactive isotope of carbon present in all living beings, begins to decrease at the moment of death. Because we also know that radioactive carbon has a half-life of around 5,500 years, we are able to cal-culate the date of death.'

'Ah! Well, for once, things sound quite simple and easy!'

'Pfft! You wish. It's far from simple. First, radioactive carbon has a rather large margin of error because you need a sizeable sample of organic matter to assess its presence. Moreover, the sample must not be contaminated by other organic matter, either contemporary or ancient. In other words, you must be lucky enough to excavate an adequate amount of organic matter that has not been adulterated by anything else during the intervening period. Once you retrieve it, you must imme-diately seal it to ensure that it is not contaminated by anything in the current environment, and send it directly to the labora-tory. Given that archaeological sites are very rarely comprised of layers that have remained completely undisturbed, and the organic matter retrieved is both rare and small in quantity (not surprising given that organic matter – wood, flesh, skin, etc. – has the unfortunate habit of decomposing, with the exception of some extraordinary cases), you get a sense of how difficult it is to actually bring this kind of dating to fruition. Additionally, radioactive carbon does not give you an actual date. Oh no, no such luck! What it gives you is a chronological range – from date x to date y – that can range from 50 to 100 or even 200 years. Granted, when we're in prehistory, it makes little difference if something is dated at 5330 BCE or 5270 BCE, but when we get to the historic period, one or two hundred years makes a huge difference. Therefore, yes, radioactive carbon is a great boon, but it's only useful if and when it is located in adequately sized samples, provides a small range of values, and, chiefly, concerns prehistoric antiquities. Despite all this, it does give us a somewhat broad but indicative chronology.'

'Are there any other dating methods?'

'Another common method is dendrochronology. You remember how at school we were taught that trees produce a new growth ring each year? Well, when you excavate a piece of wood, it can provide the opportunity to study its annual growth rings and compare them to the pattern of rings from other trees in the area. In doing so, you may be able to determine the date of the tree. Indeed, after years of research, we now have adequate data from trees throughout the Mediterranean and Europe, stretching over thousands of years. Of course, in order to be able to use this dating method, you need to be lucky enough to find a sample of wood well-preserved enough to retain its growth ring pattern. In Greece, this is a rare occurrence, because, as I've already explained, wood deteriorates relatively easily. As is probably obvious, absolute dating is generally a difficult feat, which is why archaeologists mainly rely on the relative method.'

'Got it. So that's why you said the Dark Ages, and not 1050 BCE.'

'Exactly.'

'OK, then, let's move on. Something happened, and Mycenaean civilisation went belly-up. What came next?'

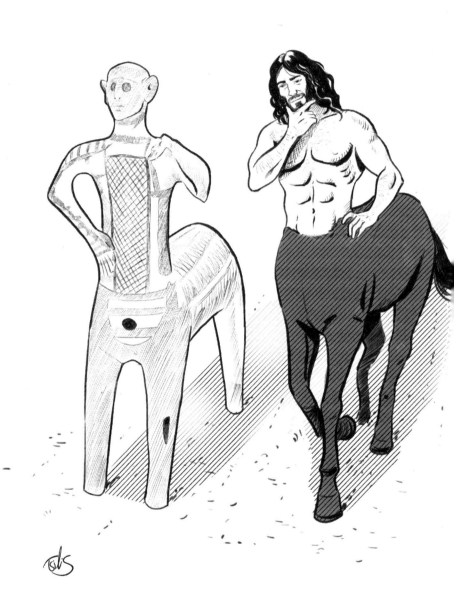

5

Yesterday
(The Dark Ages)

'A COMPLETE COLLAPSE, and darkness and destruction everywhere, is that it? The palaces, the walls, the prosperity – all were lost?'

'Well, the world definitely changed. People retained some of the cultural advancements of former times, but we see massive depopulation, with the number of settlements declining dramatically due to large numbers of relocations.'

'Where did people go?'

'To the northern Aegean, the shores of Asia Minor, Cyprus, and even as far as the coasts of Phoenicia and Palestine. The inhabitants of mainland Greece regress to less complicated ways of life, and the achievements of the Bronze Age are lost. They stop using the palatial writing systems that we've talked about; they stop building solid dwellings and robust walls made out of enormous slabs of rock. Even if some people still remember the glories of the past, they're unlikely to muster the manpower needed to build something as grandiose. In any case, there's no need to build like that now – the great palaces have been destroyed; they're things of the past. Now, it's every man for himself. Still, iron suddenly becomes all the rage, which is why we describe this period as the beginning of the Iron Age. Once again, ceramics help us make sense of this tumultuous time. After the Mycenaean period, we see the development of a style of ceramics decorated in geometric shapes that we call the Protogeometric style, because it preceded the advent of the Geometric style about a century and a half later.'

'Hmm ... didn't you just tell me that the Mycenaean period was followed directly by the Dark Ages?'

'It's one and the same period. The Dark Ages are also known as the Protogeometric period.'

'Archaeology is all about the catchy names, isn't it?'

'You're not wrong! In any case, Protogeometric ceramics bear a certain resemblance to those of the Mycenaean period in the types of patterns used, but you no longer see the creativity and artistry that distinguished the variety of palatial vessels. The later exemplars have large quantities of black paint covering their surfaces and a few paltry geometric shapes as decoration.'

'OK, but I still don't understand why this period is called the Dark Ages.'

'Because at one time we didn't know much about what happened after the fall of Mycenaean civilisation, so, like true novices, we decided to call this period the Greek Dark Ages. Thankfully, we know a lot more about this period now. At one time, for example, we thought that people lived in cultural stagnation for several centuries, but we now know that they began to bounce back relatively quickly. Certainly, the period saw enormous changes and upheaval: forget everything you knew about Greece at that time. When the entire social system collapses at once, and not only in Greece but throughout most of what was then the developed world, humanity's only priority is to survive and save itself.'

'Ah, like those zombie apocalypse movies! All the survivors gathered together in makeshift camps to defend themselves.'

'More or less. Very vaguely. There were no zombies in the picture, that's for sure. With the centralised power of the former palaces now gone, Hellenic space split up and separated into ethnic groups whose only goal was survival. Besides, gone were the fearsome Wanaxes and Lawagetes and the entire palatial kit and caboodle. Most likely the only leader to step into their shoes was the basileus, that lowly official who took the position of king, and this led to the gradual evolution of the term's significance.'

'Ah, I see, and so "king" becomes the term for the most powerful leader.'

'Splintered and true to the motto "every man for himself", these ethnic groups struggled for their survival in a variety of different ways, depending on their location. In Crete, for example, we find settlements vastly different from the large urban centres of the former period. Now, tiny villages cling to the sides of steep, rocky mountains for both concealment and protection. People on mainland Greece, on the other hand, begin to move. This is the first great migration that led to the first wave of Greek colonialism. Various Greek ethnic groups cross the Hellenic space and make their way to the islands and even the shores of Asia Minor, occupying lands where they remain settled through the historic period.'

'What are these Greek ethnic groups you're talking about?'

'There were many. The largest were the Dorians and the Ionians. The Dorians settled mainly in the Peloponnese, the southern Aegean Islands, Crete, and the southern shores of Asia Minor. The Ionians were in the central Aegean, Attica, and the central shores of Asia Minor. The Aeolians were another fairly large ethnic group that spread across the northern shores of Asia Minor. There were also a number of other smaller groups scattered throughout the Hellenic space.'

'How long did all this chaos last?'

'As I said, it didn't take long for the people to bounce back. The most impressive archaeological discovery of that period – once again evidence of the way that archaeology always surprises us – was in Lefkandi in Euboea: a monumental, long, and narrow building of almost 500 square metres in size, with many different rooms, and possibly a second floor. The most significant find, however, was a large mound in the centre of the building that held the graves of a man and a woman.'

'Who were they? Local potentates? A king and queen?'

'Yes, quite right, it's likely that they were a married royal couple. They had been buried along with a number of horses and many opulent grave goods.'

'What are grave goods?'

'It's the term we use in archaeology to describe items that are buried with a body as gifts or offerings. Anyway, in this case, many of the grave goods found were not Greek, but had been imported. Therefore, although we had once considered this period to be a dark, benighted, culturally stagnant time, we were able to deduce that not only did it have its monumental buildings – albeit few in number – but also riches and relative prosperity. It might not have been one of those Malibu villas in California right next to Hollywood's movie stars, but Lefkandi is a far from unattractive place.'

'True. And it's by the seaside and has a wonderful beach – so eat your heart out, Hollywood!'

'Lefkandi had even greater surprises in store for us. It

revealed the origins of the folk traditions that laid the foundations for the creation of the Greek myths. A case in point: the clay figurine of a centaur found in a young girl's grave. Even though it is the most ancient figurine of a centaur found to date, this is not the most interesting fact about it. This centaur is connected to the myth of Chiron, the only centaur to stand out as an individual, whose wisdom and love of justice helped him train many ancient heroes in the art of medicine.'

'Why was Chiron the only centaur to stand out?'

'The centaurs were wild, violent, and generally disorderly types; utter delinquents. Chiron, in contrast, was a cut above: wise, kind, a real gentleman – a gentleman on hooves.'

'Sounds like the title to a romantic comedy! How do we know that the centaur found at that burial site was Chiron?'

'According to myth, Heracles mistakenly wounded Chiron in the leg, and the figurine found in the girl's grave has a leg wound! What's even more interesting, though—'

'Goodness, there's no end to it.'

'The centaur was found in pieces. One piece was found in the girl's grave, the other in a neighbouring grave. We don't know why. The two graves and their owners were probably related, and this figurine surely had some significance for both.'

'Wow! I've never heard about this site. Why isn't it better-known? Are you archaeologists trying to keep it all to yourselves?'

'Oh, don't start with that old chestnut again. Archaeologist aren't interested in hiding information; in fact, we make sure to shout it from the rooftops so that everyone has access to it.'

'Yet now you're telling me that Euboea in the Dark Ages was actually quite advanced!'

'Don't let it fool you, though. The finds at Lefkandi do not mean that Greece in 1000 BCE was awash with Kim Kardashian types strutting around their manor houses in their expensive imported jewellery. Besides, even the monumental building in Lefkandi I mentioned earlier was made out of timber and adobe, had a straw roof, and looked more like a large stable than a grand manor. What the finds do prove is that people knew how to make long journeys, and that they never lost their connection to the outside world, despite the fact that the Hellenic world was now utterly provincial when compared to the great eastern civilisations.'

'And people's lives back then, what were they like?'

'Most regular folk lived in dwellings that were similar to what we would describe today as wooden shepherd's cabins. Anywhere where timber was available, that is, because on the islands, where it was scarce, they were built from stone. The dwellings were heaped right next to each other along narrow lanes, crammed within the walls that protected the settlement from outside marauders. The chieftain's dwelling would have been a tad larger than the rest – a real big shot, that one! Here and there among the general jumble, there'd be a vacant plot, either used for community events or dedicated to a god. In those early days, you see, the gods were worshipped out in the open air, in a space that had been designated for this purpose alone, separated out from human spaces – remember our discussion of that Linear B word, *temno*?'

'Yes, from the Mycenaean period! Were they still worshipping the pantheon of gods you mentioned earlier? I remember you also said that the twelve Olympians have been kicking around since then – Zeus, Poseidon, Hera, Demeter, Aphrodite, Athena, Artemis, Apollo, Ares, Hephaestus, Hermes, and Dionysus?'

'That's right! That's when the worship of the Olympian gods began to take the mould that it retained for some time to come. During the Dark or Protogeometric Ages, then, the most likely scenario is that all the gods were worshipped in nature, and all nature was considered divine; in fact, one might say that the image of the divine was everywhere, the sky, the earth, the sea, the trees. Some trees even brought to mind the human figure, and even when they didn't, trees gave so much – shade, nourishment – yet the poor things shrivelled and seemed to die each year, only to be reborn several months later. How could they not be divine? So people created likenesses of the gods as they imagined them, and as they were able to with their hands, in one way or another; sometimes using metal, or, more commonly, wood – indeed, some pieces of wood resembled the human trunk of their own accord. They erected them in the village centre, where they worshipped the divine powers in the hopes that they would show them mercy and allow them to survive another winter or another enemy raid. Not to mention that, one day, they might take sick, and their usual elixirs and herbs might not work. In fact, in general, they lived such very difficult lives that they believed that the gods who presided over them must also be hard and difficult beings who needed to be appeased, mollified, brought around. Those symbols of the gods had to be protected at all costs, so they built a shelter around each to shield them from the winds and the rain and the hail. A little cabin of sorts, a dwelling – a house of the god. This is how, somehow or other, we get to the origins of temple-building, and many of those early, rudimentary "statues" of the gods become cult images that are watched over and honoured for many centuries to come. In any case, because nothing ever remains static in human history, as I've already mentioned, it was only a matter of time before the mists of the Dark Ages began to clear.'

'I have another question.'

'Shoot.'

'I've been mulling it over for some time.'

'Go on, then.'

'It's not directly related to what you were talking about.'

'Oh, for God's sake, ask!'

'Before you started talking about Lefkandi, you told me about the fall of civilisations, and somewhere along the way you mentioned differences of opinion about human sacrifice in Crete. You often touch on the fact that there are many divergent opinions among researchers. So, tell me . . . why is archaeology so contentious?'

FAQ

Why is Archaeology So Contentious?

'BECAUSE YOU CAN'T have a discipline without disagreement. Disciplines, after all, exist on a global scale, and humans can't even agree about which side of the road we ought to drive on globally, the right or the left. Why do you expect unanimity on disciplinary matters?'

'OK, fair point, but I thought scholars were educated and cultured people. Can't they reach an agreement?'

'Disagreement is at the heart of scholarship. It is what sets archaeology apart from the sterility and barrenness of a slavish worship of the past. In fact, it is the only way that we can test the hypotheses that drive our research, to verify them and determine whether they hold any water.'

'I don't understand what you mean.'

'In the humanities, disagreement helps us test our theories and conduct our research studies. This is how it works: a researcher presents a working theory, an idea, a case-study, and the rest of the scholarly community then examines it. This occurs only when the researcher's work is published in its entirety, with all the thinking and scientific data behind it. In this fundamental scientific process, the disagreements that inevitably arise help us check and recheck all the data. Essentially, these disagreements are akin to the clinical trials that take place before a new medicine is released to the public. Because, no matter what, unanimous agreement is well-nigh impossible, we need a majority agreement before something is broadly adopted by the discipline. There are always a handful of naysayers, even to the most basic of principles.'

'What is archaeology's biggest controversy?'

'It's impossible to compare. In Greek archaeology, a well-known controversial issue is the date for the eruption of the Santorini volcano, which at one point was estimated to have occurred at around 1450 BCE. It turns out that the eruption most likely dates to approximately two centuries earlier and falls between three possible timeframes, 1628 to 1642 BCE, 1642 to 1616 BCE, or 1664 to 1651 BCE. You see what I'm getting at, don't you? There have also been longstanding disagreements about the identity of the occupant of Royal Tomb II at Vergina, whom most archaeologists believe to be Philip II of Macedon, Alexander the Great's father. Others, however, maintain that it is in fact his half-brother, Arrhidaeus, who assumed the name Philip when he ascended to the throne.'

'Couldn't they have written "here lies so and so" on their tombs and be done with it?'

'Yes, the fact that there are no inscriptions on the tomb does make things difficult, but keep in mind that out of all of ancient Macedonia's royal and elite tombs – approximately 130 have been found to date – only two have inscriptions with the names of their occupants. Even if Royal Tomb II bore an inscription, however, it would most likely say "Philip", so it would be virtually useless given that both contenders went by that name.'

'I see. But these are big and weighty issues, and I imagine there's not as much disagreement about less important ones. What would be the point?'

'We don't disagree about everything, but we can definitely disagree about *anything*, no matter how small. Let's look at another, less well-known, example: the Necromanteion of Acheron in Epirus in north-west Greece. This ancient temple of necromancy devoted to Hades was frequented by the faithful who wished for an oracle not from a god, like Zeus at Dodona, or Apollo at Delphi, but from the dead in the Underworld. A thoroughly terrifying situation, in other words. It was no easy feat to breach the boundary between this life and the next. The Necromanteion that survives today resembles a fortified tower. Our excavations revealed rooms that were thought to serve as dormitories for pilgrims who had travelled to see the oracle of the dead. We found large urns containing the remnants of foodstuffs like grains and pulses – broad beans featured prominently – that are generally thought to cause hallucinations. The faithful, you see, were required to fast and follow a special diet that got them high as kites. We also found a twisting corridor with various gates, like a small labyrinth, that led to a hole in the ground and ended in a dark, damp, and frightening inner sanctum with a domed ceiling. That's where the pilgrims, woolly-headed from fasting, strange food, and the twists and turns of the corridor, were received by the alleged spirits of the dead, flickering in front of them as they delivered their oracles. What's truly mind-blowing is that we found cogs and other parts of a type of crane that were interpreted as the remnants of a mechanism used to animate puppets that played the role of dead spirits for the befuddled audiences. The hapless pilgrims, stomachs like drums from the gourmet meals they'd been fed at the temple – not a Michelin star in sight! – were completely rattled, and took the shapes flickering before their eyes as spirits risen before them from the beyond!'

'OK, so what was the disagreement?'

'That everything I've just told you is based on an incorrect interpretation of the finds. The entire Necromanteion complex was surrounded by high fortification walls like a fortress. Ceramics and other finds at the site suggest that the final phase of its use had taken place immediately prior to the Roman conquest of Epirus. As we know, Epirus was conquered by the Romans after great bloodshed: seventy cities and settlements were destroyed and 150,000 inhabitants were taken as slaves.'

'You mean to say that the building was not a temple, but a fortress?'

'One theory is that it was among the last fortresses standing in the defence of Epirus against the Roman onslaught. The large urns are therefore explained by the necessity for food storage during a siege, and the cogs and other metal bits and pieces as parts of the fortress's defensive weaponry – like a trebuchet, for example. As for the inner sanctum, the hypothesis is that it was a plain old cellar.'

'So which interpretation is correct?'

'Everything I've just told you makes sense, except for the fact that it does not explain the need for that twisting corridor in the building. I mean, you're already under siege, do you really need to navigate a labyrinth on top of it? Unless you're a masochist, it's a complete mystery. The theory also doesn't explain why the alleged cellar was built with such attention to detail, arches and all. In fact, an extended examination of the space – whether we consider it a cellar or the portal to the Underworld – revealed that it functioned like an anechoic chamber.'

'What in God's name is that?'

'It was designed not to reflect sound. In other words, there was no echo, and it could maintain an almost perfect silence.'

'Alright, but it's feasible that the cogs actually did belong to a trebuchet?'

'Yes, of course. The fact that the Necromanteion may have been used as a fortress in the resistance to the invasion, however, does not mean that it had not earlier functioned as a temple.'

'Fair enough. So what was the outcome of all this debate?'

'New research corroborates the theory that the site was indeed a temple of necromancy. What do we learn from this example? That challenges to a prevailing theory are necessary as catalysts for more research and analysis, to either prove the challenging theory or to bolster the original theory with more robust arguments and data. Ta-da! This is why disagreement is so necessary to the discipline.'

'OK, that's all great . . . but tell me something – are we ever going to get to classical Greece? All this time, and we're still in prehistory.'

'We're getting there.'

6

You Spin Me Round
(The Geometric Age)

'DRUM ROLL, PLEASE, for the Geometric period that paved the way for classical antiquity's cultural miracle! When, finally, the Hellenic space emerges from the darkness, a new world awaits.'

'Remind me again why it's called the Geometric period?'

'Because of the ceramics. What do the vases of this period look like? They're absolutely covered in geometric motifs! In the preceding period, large surfaces remained unadorned. Now, not only are the motifs themselves larger, but the entire vase is decorated.'

'And besides the ceramics, what else changed?'

'A great many things. The population of Geometric Greece is divided into small political units that will eventually grow into city-states. The economy changes as trade flourishes. Ceramics production improves, and the use of iron becomes widespread. In fact, we are now in a period when new "technologies", in the broad sense of the word, begin to take their first tentative steps.'

'Just a sec. When you were talking about the previous period, you repeatedly mentioned Euboea. Was it still a centre of power and influence at this time?'

'In the very early historic age, and specifically the Geometric period that we are now talking about, there was no single centre of power. It is true, of course, that Athens begins to take the lead, and its artistic production, in particular its pottery, attests to this. In fact, Athens was at the forefront of the Geometric style and inspired many other imitations and adaptations.'

'You mean to say that there were various styles of pottery throughout Greece?'

'Yes, a number of other cities developed their own individual styles, yet the influence of Athenian pottery throughout Greece is remarkable. We see the creation of enormous, human-sized vases that were used as funerary markers. These too were chock-a-block with symmetrical and exceptionally precise geometric motifs. Not an inch of the vase remained unadorned, which is why we say that the artists of that time suffered from *horror vacui*, a fear of empty spaces. It was as if they were possessed and could not stop working until they had left their mark all over the vase.'

'Did they use only geometric motifs? What about human figures? A couple of old geezers, at least?'

'Yes – step by uncertain step, they began to create the first representations of humans, animals, and chiefly funerals.'

'Why funerals?' He asked, spitting and crossing his fingers superstitiously.

'Don't forget that most of the vases that we have today endured precisely because they played a role in burial rites. The larger ones functioned as monumental grave markers, and the smaller ones were placed inside the tomb as offerings. This is what preserved them for us through the centuries, and as a result we've been able to study them closely, and have even begun to recognise the hand of different artists. In fact, we've given them names: the Dipylon Master, the Hirschfeld Painter, and so on and so forth.'

'So it's all about the pottery again?'

'They're among the most important relics of that period.'

'OK, but I also have some very basic questions about what you said earlier concerning the evolution of the Hellenic world that led to classical Greek culture. How did that all begin?'

'It began in the regions inhabited by enterprising souls who were drawn to travel and trade: Euboea, Crete, and the islands of the eastern Aegean. If we look at Euboea, for example, surely the fierce competition between the neighbouring cities of Chalkida and Eretria that had them locked in a struggle for dominance played a determinative role. Rather than sit there spinning their wheels, the adventurers among them boarded ship and took to sea! At some point, a particularly bright spark catches sight of something curious that's happening yonder, in the environs of Phoenicia in the more advanced east: they're using a writing system with a limited number of symbols. He takes it and adapts it, adding vowels, amending the consonants so that they better conform to the Greek language, thus creating the world's first writing system that pairs a letter to every sound made in human speech, be it a consonant or a vowel. This is how the Greeks went from having forgotten writing for centuries – and a writing system that was cumbersome and arcane – to possessing a tool that radically changed their culture.'

'Big deal! They invented an alphabet. So what?'

'Oh, no, my friend, you're mistaken! This invention was world-altering in its simplicity: a phonetically correct alphabet consisting, all in all, of a couple of dozen letters that was simple enough to be easily learned and versatile enough to fully capture complex thoughts and the idiosyncrasy of the individual voice. The repercussions were unimaginable. For one, this new alphabet gradually paved the way for the miracle of ancient Greek culture by facilitating a much broader dissemination of information than had been previously possible. It was the fertile soil that nurtured the seeds of self-determination, the transmission of knowledge, the flourishing of philosophy, arts, and all other branches of knowledge; even the birth of democracy.'

'Earlier, when we were talking about Linear B, you said that it was used to record the palace accounts. Was this new writing system any different?'

'Completely. In fact, there's something really wonderful about this early Greek writing that is usually overlooked: most extant ancient Greek scripts are in verse – poetry, in other words.'

'They were writing poetry? Are you having me on?'

'Not at all. Poetry was one of the first things written with the new Greek alphabet. You see, once again, art leads the way! As soon, then, as people began to transcribe their thoughts and speeches so that someone, somewhere, in a distant place or time might read them, the entire world changed. The ephemerality of the spoken word was replaced by the permanence of the visual symbol. What we don't yet know much about is how this early Greek alphabet split into a range of local variants. Of course, one of the most remarkable things about this alphabet is that soon after its discovery and dissemination, two of the most enduring bestsellers in global literature, the *Iliad* and the *Odyssey*, are created.'

'You mean they were written back then?'

'Although those particular poems were not "written down"

then, we do know that they were created at that time. I just want to illustrate how important and popular poetrywas in that period. Epic poetry, after all, was performed by itinerant bards and was meant to be sung throughout the Greek world. Indeed, these epics have fired the human imagination for approximately 3,000 years and are known the world over; I reckon they have inspired more artists, writers, and performers than any other works of art! Besides, the Homeric epics are absolutely brilliant stories that were renowned from the moment of their creation. They're full of gripping scenes that continue to thrill and move us to this day.'

'I guess I'll have to take your word for it.'

'Oh, come on, do you really need convincing? There are so many outstanding passages, I don't know where to begin. There's the part in the *Iliad*, for example, where Achilles, mourning the death of his beloved Patroclus, requests replacement armour from Hephaestus and returns to battle to wreak his revenge. He massacres so many Trojans that the river Scamander, running red with their blood, rises up to do battle with the mythical hero.'

'Was Homer famous even back then, or are we the ones to have discovered him and showered him with accolades?'

'Homer never lost his popularity. He was the ultimate bestseller! He's not one of those artists who belongs to the ivory towers of academia. Instead, he is part of the popular traditions that produced his epics. Even our grandparents, a generation that didn't have the educational opportunities we enjoy today (I mean, some of them didn't even go to school), know about Odysseus and Achilles. Homer was always a product of the popular tradition, and so he remains.'

'Greek folk art, you mean?'

'Yes, but of the epic variety! Have you any idea how catchy his epics were? They are complicated tales replete with plot twists and narrative tricks that continue to captivate. Let's look, for example, at the structure of the *Odyssey*. It begins without preamble near the end of the plot, with Odysseus, the archetypal daredevil, languishing on Calypso's island. Having survived a series of misadventures, he is now hiding from Poseidon, who is looking to wreak vengeance on him. Simultaneously, we learn of the goings-on in Ithaca, Odysseus's failing kingdom, where his wife, Penelope, and son are struggling to keep things afloat until his return while also fending off her suitors. From the very beginning of the narrative, then, we find ourselves slap-bang in the middle of a very complicated situation. We are forced to ask ourselves how Odysseus got to where he is, and how and if he will manage to unravel the mess. At one point, when Poseidon is absent, the other gods intervene, having decided to allow Odysseus to return home. Odysseus, too, has concocted a plan for his return. But will he make it?'

'There's a plot twist, isn't there?'

'Poseidon returns and calls down a horrific storm that leads to one of my favourite episodes in the narrative: the minor goddess Leucothea offers the shipwrecked Odysseus her veil to keep him afloat in the furious waves until Athena comes to the rescue. In the end, he is saved at the eleventh hour and washes up on the island of the Phaeacians. Nothing has yet been resolved; we are still only in the middle of this thrilling ride. Odysseus must now explain all his preceding adventures to the Phaeacians in an attempt to ingratiate himself and earn their help. That's when the flashbacks – pure drama and action! – begin: there's the Cyclops Polyphemus, Circe, Scylla and Charybdis, the Laestrygonians, the Lotus-eaters, the descent to the Underworld. After listening to this rollercoaster, the Phaeacians help Odysseus get to Ithaca. Is that the end of the story? Of course not. Just like a screenwriter at the end of a thriller, Homer throws even more hurdles in Odysseus's way as he attempts to regain his throne. He has to disguise himself as a beggar and use his cunning to defeat his numerous and formidable foes. By the time the curtain falls, however, the story has come to its happy conclusion for both Odysseus and the audience. Don't forget that this is not a contemporary script, but the most ancient fantasy-adventure tale ever written.'

'Do Homer's epics accurately depict the period in which they were written? After all, he mentions Troy, Mycenae – all the great heroes.'

'No, not even close! It's a huge mistake to read Homer as a mirror of the period. His work contains an amalgam of references to Mycenaean and Geometric cultures, and is not a trustworthy guide to historical reality. Besides, don't forget that the epics are creative works of poetry, not historiography.'

'But we've found Troy, Mycenae – even the palaces belonging to the heroes he mentions.'

'We've found archaeological sites that most likely were named Troy, Mycenae, etc., and probably inspired the creation of the myths. This, however, does not mean that the myth itself has been fully authenticated. For example, we can't even prove that the tomb we identify as the Tomb of Agamemnon is actually his.'

'You know what? You're reminding me that our high-school literature teacher once told us that Homer did not exist. She said that the epics had been composed by a number of different poets, and were combined after the fact. What do you say to that?'

'Yes, that's the Homeric conundrum: were the epics composed by many poets or just one? If Homer was the one, when did he compose them? And so on and so forth. Let's put aside, though, the scholarly slanging matches and the rivalries and controversies that have come from poring over the *Iliad* and the *Odyssey*. What's important is that the Homeric epics were and have remained a cornerstone of culture and learning, the foundation of a classical education.'

'Well, I certainly never dreamed that a humble Greek alphabet would be used from the outset to document something as important as poetry.'

'This ought to sober you up a bit: not all inscriptions, especially the most ancient ones, were of such a fine calibre. In fact, ancient Greeks would write, or, to be fully accurate, engrave, anything you can possibly imagine on their pottery. Inscriptions of ownership, for example, were very common.'

'You mean like how we write our names on our belongings: "this belongs to so and so"?'

'Exactly. One of the most ancient and famous Greek inscriptions is engraved on a cup that originally hailed from Rhodes but was found on a tiny island in the Gulf of Naples, off the coast of Italy. (Yes, the Greeks travelled, and so did their things!) The cup reads: "I am the cup of Nestor, good for drinking. Whoever drinks from this cup will be seized instantly by the desire of beautifully crowned Aphrodite."'

'What is this desire of beautifully crowned Aphrodite?'

'Are you seriously asking me what "the desire of Aphrodite" means? She is the goddess of love.'

'Oh!'

'Exactly what came to mind right then.'

'But wait . . . this is supposed to be the cup talking?'

'Yes! Because back then they believed that all objects had souls, the inscriptions were written in the voice of the objects on which they were engraved. There's another inscription, one of the most ancient we've retrieved, from Methone in Pieria, that not only declares who the cup belongs to, but also issues a threat: "Whoever steals me", it reads, "will lose his eyes." A cup from Massalia warns, "I belong to Ariston. Put me down. Let me be! Walk away."'

'Wow! It sounds like the inscriptions were all threats!'

'No, of course not! It's true that given our turbulent histories, we Mediterranean types can be temperamental drama queens; when all is said and done, though, revelry, high spirits, and love have always prevailed. Which is to say that we also have inscriptions that are much more free-wheeling and happy-go-lucky. A good example is the one on an Athenian wine jug, or oinochoe, announcing that whoever among the dancers manages to dance *atalotata* (that is the exact word) will get the jug as a trophy.'

'What does that word *atalotata* mean?'

'It's such a wonderful ancient Greek word that I can't find a good equivalent. It means the utmost tenderness and grace of youth.'

'Where were they dancing?'

'In this particular case, probably at a symposium, because it is around this time in Greek history when we see the inauguration of this famous institution, where, in addition to their revelries, they were entertained by competitions. Hence the inscription on the vase-trophy, "this vase will go to the best dancer". Another inscription exhorts us to unwind: "Drink, slake your thirst, live"; while yet another declares itself the gift of a lovestruck soul: "Mogeas has given me as a gift to Efcharis, so that she may drink to her heart's content".'

'Aww! It sounds like Geometric Greece was a riot! Tell me, though, is it considered part of prehistory, or history?'

'During the Geometric period, ancient Greece finally enters the historic period. The official cut-off date is 776 BCE.'

'Why couldn't they just round it up? Did something really important happen that year?'

'Yes. The first Olympic Games at ancient Olympia! The Geometric period is when both the first Panhellenic sanctuaries – Apollo's in Delos, Demeter's in Eleusis, Zeus's in Olympia – and the first oracles – Zeus's in Dodona and Apollo's in Delphi – are founded. Also, as I just mentioned, the Olympic Games are launched. Even though initially quite small in scale, they soon become the number one event in the ancient world.'

'You know what? I read somewhere that in ancient Greece the audience would throw clothes at the winner of the games. Is that true?'

'OK, listen . . . this is a good opportunity to clarify something.'

FAQ

Did They Do This, That or the Other in Ancient Greece?
The 'Worst' Kind of Questions?

'WHAT DID THEY EAT in ancient Greece? What was the lifestyle like in ancient Greece? Did they believe or do x, y, or z in ancient Greece?

'Any archaeologist engaged in conversation about antiquity will have come across questions like these. Unfortunately, they are questions based on a rather shaky premise. They have no idea what they mean by "ancient Greece". Most of the time, they probably mean Athens during the classical era, which is not surprising given that classical Athens represents the pinnacle of ancient Greek culture and the overwhelming majority of surviving textual sources come from that period. Antiquity, however, was neither a discrete nor a static point in time. On the contrary, it comprises a long, extended period characterised by constant and complex change on all levels: cultural, social, geographic, and so on. Accordingly, any question concerning ancient Greece *in general* is based on a misconception. What do you mean by "ancient Greece"? Which of its many versions are you referring to?'

'There were many versions?'

'When you talk about ancient Greece, do you mean Euboea in the tenth century BCE – we already mentioned Lefkandi with its remarkable finds – when it had resumed trade with the Near East and new ideas and influences were flooding into the Hellenic world? Or do you mean the city of Argos in the ninth century, with its aristocratic knights astride their horses? Or is it Sparta in the eighth century, which was in the process of forming a military regime under a highly unusual double monarchy? (Yes, Sparta, in that period, had two kings of equal standing, who would split the role during times of war with one serving as leader of the army and the other remaining in charge of the city.) Or might it be the island of Samos in the seventh century, with its opulent harbour and its renowned, exceedingly wealthy sanctuary for Hera that drew pilgrims from around the world? There's also, of course, Athens in the sixth century, and the social upheaval that led Cleisthenes to reform the constitution and pave the path to democracy. Or the northern Greek kingdom of Macedonia in the fifth century, with its agrarian communities and its semi-nomadic horse and cattle herders roaming the mountains, while the Macedonian monarchs of the Argead dynasty fought their wars of succession and tried to build bridges with southern Greece. Or the island of Rhodes of the fourth century, with its wealthy harbours and schools of art that produced the most renowned artists and sculptors of the period.'

'I see what you mean.'

'There are big and important cultural, political, and social differences among the periods and places I just mentioned. Ancient Greece is neither a fixed nor monolithic landscape. So yes, all sorts of things took place during this sweeping and heterogeneous period of time, and not only can we trace some of them back to prehistory, but some are prevalent for the duration of antiquity.'

'Like? Can you give me an example?'

'Worship in a Pantheon, for one. In fact, to this day, we have customs, like the ritual feasting on grilled meats, that can be traced to antiquity, when such grilling would take place after sacrifices to the gods; today, of course, it is an integral part of Easter Sunday celebrations – all that lamb roasting on the spit! Another example is the Greek custom of naming the first grandson after the paternal grandfather to ensure the continuation of the name. Conversely, there were also plenty of practices that were confined to particular places and times. And no need to ask, because I've got you covered: in ancient Sparta, both boys and girls were expected to follow physical fitness regimes and attend gymnasiums. Here's a weird one: ancient Macedonians would tear a female dog in two and have their troops march in procession between the two parts as a form of ritual cleansing of the army before battle.'

'Are you telling me that these questions are meaningless?'

'I didn't say that! They are reasonable, meaningful, and often a lot more substantial than questions about chronology. My point is that we ought not to file all the information we have about antiquity under the same tab and the same period. For instance, you would never say that, in twentieth-century Greece, the telegram was the most common method of long-distance communication, or that people would use the corner kiosk to make a call because most homes did not have a telephone. Just as you also couldn't say that most people used mobile phones. Not because everything I've just mentioned does not apply, but rather because it does not apply to the twentieth century *as a whole*. This is what I mean when I warn of the dangers of overgeneralising antiquity.

'As for what you mentioned earlier about the audience throwing clothes at the winners of the games: yes, at some point in antiquity, they did do that. Offered as gifts and signs of admiration, it was customary to cover the winning athlete with clothes. But it was not a custom that lasted very long.'

7

Light My Fire
(The Archaic Period)

'So, are we finally there? We're done with the Geometric period and are now in the Classical, correct?'

'No! First, we need to get through the very important Archaic period, named that way because it directly precedes the Classical. Essentially, it led the way, cleaned the house, cooked, and put its feet up for a while before rolling out the carpets and getting everything ready for the Classical period to don the wreath of victory and take all the glory. In short, the Archaic period laid the foundations for Greek antiquity's classical miracle.'

'Interesting. But first explain when all this happened, and how long it lasted.'

'The Archaic period extends from 700 BCE to about 500 BCE, although we can draw it out a little longer, to approximately 480 BCE, to the time of the Persian Wars and the definitive defeat of the Persian Empire, the region's imperialist bruisers at the time.'

'What were the important developments of the Archaic period?'

'The ancient Greeks' fascination with the Near East exerted

a great influence on the development of the culture. After gruel-ling, turbulent journeys across the Mediterranean on fast and agile ships, they would dock at foreign harbours, their gateways to the cities of Phoenicia, Assyria, Egypt, and other states with already developed civilisations. There, they would visit the city bazaars and markets, the temples with their enormous statues of foreign gods, and take in the thick walls carved with reliefs, the woven and knitted textiles, the cookware and tableware of both fine and everyday varieties, all covered in a riot of dec-oration: abstract motifs, finely painted tableaux, animals both existent and imaginary – lions, leopards, deer, eagles, sphinxes, griffins, roosters, goats – as well as human figures, of course. Floral patterns were used to fill the dead spaces.'

'They were impressed by the bazaars and cultures of the Near East, then?'

'Very much so! Those Greek travellers were both envious of what they saw and inspired by it, and, over time, they began to assimilate those near-eastern motifs and styles, and reproduce them on Greek artefacts. As a result, the prevailing Geometric style was replaced by a broader range of ornamental and fig-urative motifs that included animals, flowers, human figures – you name it, they had it! This period, when foreign influences played such a determinative role in Greek art and culture, is known as the Orientalising period.'

'Wait a sec . . . from the Geometric we went to the Archaic . . . and now we're in the Orientalising period. Does that mean that we're already done with the Archaic?'

'No, the Orientalising period is a relatively brief interlude in the history of Greek art that occurred between the Geometric and the Archaic. We're essentially talking about the first few decades of the Archaic period.'

'All these periods and sub-periods will be the death of me!'

'But this one is super important! It was the kick in the pants that the Greeks of the seventh century BCE needed to begin the experimentation that led directly to the Archaic period.'

'OK, but besides the art, what else happened? What was life like during the Archaic period?'

'The Greek mainland had already splintered into hundreds of city-states that now began to take their definitive form.'

'Hang on. What do you mean by the "definitive form of a city-state"?'

'Essentially, I am talking about an independent fortified city with a basic public infrastructure – agora (a public gathering space, assembly place or market place), temples, gymnasiums – and contiguous cultivable land beyond the city walls, which was used to grow the grains, fruit, and vegetables needed to feed its citizens.'

'Were there many of these city-states?'

'Hundreds. Keep in mind that in antiquity, there were hundreds of different state units throughout Greece. Most were city-states, especially in southern Greece, the islands, and the coast of Asia Minor. There were also a handful of surviving kingdoms, like Macedonia, Epirus, and Thessaly, and several tribal communities in the mountain regions of western Greece, that lived in more rustic conditions than the others.'

'But Greece is pocket-sized! How did it accommodate hundreds of city-states with enough surrounding land to grow their own produce?'

'That's a great point! Because of limited availability, many of these communities did not possess enough fertile land to feed all their citizens. Yet the population kept growing, and things started to get tight. And what happens when things get tight?'

'People fight.'

'Exactly. The most immediate solution was for some of the population to get the hell out. At the time, we see an upsurge of emigration to foreign parts that became known as the second wave of Greek colonisation.'

'Wait, when did the first wave happen?'

'After the fall of the Mycenaean palaces at around 1100–1050 BCE. Don't you remember? We already covered that.'

'Yeah, OK, no need to get stroppy. You only mentioned it once. Do you really expect me to remember everything?'

'Point taken. In any case, colonisation is a big deal, because it is neither simple nor easy. These people had to find a new place to live, somewhere with resources abundant enough for their sustenance, and native populations willing to coexist with them. It was not always feasible, and many attempts were unsuccessful.'

'Well, how difficult was it?'

'Let's take the ancient city-state of Thera on the island of Santorini as an example. At the time, it was overflowing with inhabitants and there was drought for good measure, so, as you can imagine, tempers flared and dissension raged. There may also have been political reasons for the conflicts, inheritance issues, land – all you need is the inclination, and if people want a fight, a fight is what they'll get. It was not long before a number of them had boarded ship in search of new lands. Their search was not unsuccessful, but for some reason they were unable to settle, so, poor souls, they had to climb back onboard their ships and return to the island. They did not receive a very friendly welcome. "Ugh! Now that we're finally able to breathe freely and have regained a measure of peace, why are this lot hauling their sorry carcasses back here?" This must have been the thought in the minds of those who had remained behind, for they rushed down to the harbour and began throwing rocks at the ships to chase them away. Once again, these beleaguered, sea-tossed souls pulled away and sailed to the shores of North Africa, where they founded Kyrene.'

'They settled there?'

'Not only did they settle there, but Kyrene grew into a large and hugely prosperous city. And this is only one of many similar migrations that took place in this period from various parts of Greece to destinations throughout the Mediterranean. Dozens of cities, both big and small, sowed colonies in the four directions of the compass. Some only a few; others, a great many. At times, we see two or more cities collaborating to found new colonies.'

'Really? They'd pair up and step up, so to speak?'

'That's right. Pithekoussai, the oldest Greek colony in southern Italy, was located on an island in the Gulf of Naples and settled by populations from Eretria and Chalkida. The same is true of another colony, Cumae, located on the mainland right across from Pithekoussai.'

'Pithekoussai? What a name! Does it come from the Greek word for ape, *pithikos*? Were there apes on the island?'

'Quite likely, although the name may also come from the word *pithos*, the large storage containers popular at the time. Sybaris, situated in modern Calabria, was founded by settlers from the region of Achaea, along with people from the city of Troezena. These types of collaborations were not uncommon. All these people relocated, abandoned hearth, home, and roots, and withstood the raging waves of change, both literally and figuratively, in order to survive in their new homelands. It stands to reason that they'd experiment with new forms of social ties and attachments. They built new states, new relationships, and this loosening of former social structures paved the way for a new era. The Greek world was in for some radical change.'

'Do you mean to say that a new spirit of collaboration prevailed? That's odd. Weren't there any conflicts at the time?'

'Of course there were. The collaborations I mentioned were exceptions. Besides, war had really changed too. In the Archaic period we see the establishment of organised warfare, with armies that include all eligible citizens and the creation of the phalanx as a tactical formation: a block of heavily armed infantry, standing shoulder-to-shoulder in lines, their shields protecting both themselves and their neighbours and forming an iron wall through which only their spears protruded. This was a new and efficient way of waging war, as well as an occasion to foster a sense of commonality and responsibility for the fate of their city among the citizenry. Besides, as Heraclitus said: πόλεμος πάντων μὲν πατήρ ἐστι, πάντων δὲ βασιλεύς. Did you understand that? It's not all that different from modern Greek.'

'You know the answer to that, mate,' he said, reprimanding me.

'Yes, yes, alright . . . it means "War is father of all, and king of all." Heraclitus was also the one who said "everything flows". He earned the epithet of the "obscure philosopher" in antiquity because his cryptic pronouncements were not immediately understood by many. In this particular quote he was probably touching on something similar to the popular idiom, "you can't make an omelette without breaking eggs".'

'What was up with philosophy? Is this when philosophy begins in ancient Greece?'

'Yes, that's right, this is when it all begins. Heraclitus was only one among a host of natural philosophers who crop up around this time: Thales, Anaximander, Anaximenes . . .'

'Where did all these characters live?'

'Have you been listening to me at all? They lived in that rich cultural and social amalgam I was just describing: the colonies of Asia Minor and southern Italy. They've been categorised into schools—'

'You mean like vocational and professional training schools?'

'Oh, for God's sake! No, of course not. I'm using "school" as a figure of speech. I mean that they were classified into groups – which we needed to do to make sense of them all, given how many of them there were – the Milesian, Ephesian, and Eleatic schools—'

'Way to go for the colonies! They changed the entire world!'

'True. Many of the colonies maintained ties to their parent city-states and built active trading networks. Corinth, in particular, lorded it over all the rest. It founded many colonies, became incredibly wealthy through its trading networks, and its ceramics were the toast of the entire Mediterranean. Indicatively, it established trade routes in two directions, with one harbour, Lechaeum, in the Corinthian Gulf to the west, for the ships that came and went through the Ionian Sea to Italy and beyond, and another harbour, Cenchreae, in the Saronic Gulf to the east, leading to the Aegean and the Near East. It's no wonder that Corinth was all boast and bluster: they knew everything there was to know about the sea. Even though it would be many centuries before the Corinth Canal was built, they had something called the *Diolkos*, a paved trackway that allowed them to transfer ships from one side of the Isthmus to the other by rolling them over three trunks.'

'That's really cool. I had no idea that the Corinthians were such seafaring types.'

'Didn't you know that according to legend, it was the Corinthian Ameinocles who invented the trireme – a ship with three rows of oars – which became the foremost warship in antiquity? There's some disagreement among ancient sources whether it was built by him as a commission for the island Samos or the city of Athens, which is not surprising, because they also disagree about whether it was, in fact, Ameinocles or some other Corinthian.'

'A little while ago, you said something about Corinthian ceramics. What was so special about them?'

'Corinthian products were distributed in beautiful clay containers that often ended up as pieces of decoration in their own right. As a result, Corinthian vessels became much sought after and Corinthian potters famous for the delicate, finely decorated work that continues to impress to this day. What's more, they invented something called the black-figure style, in which figures and motifs were painted on the vase's clay surface in a glossy black paint and the finishing details incised into it with a sharp object, producing stunning works of art. Since we've found exemplars of these vases throughout the Mediterranean, we've been able to learn a lot, not only about Corinth but also about the rest of the Greek world. One example is a particularly odd Corinthian container called an exaleiptron (from the verb meaning "to anoint") with an inward-turning lip designed to prevent spillages. They were used to store valuable essential oils, or salves and unguents. In different regions of the Greek world, in Macedonia or Rhodes for example, they were included in the burial rites, perhaps as storage for the perfumes used in the preparation of the body for its final resting place. In Corinth, however, they clearly served another function, because we haven't found any in their graves.'

'While you've been talking, I've been thinking that I only really know about two cities in ancient Greece – Athens and Sparta – yet you've barely mentioned either of them.'

'I haven't mentioned them yet because they are the two great cities that did not resort to colonisation to solve their problems, but tried instead to come up with internal solutions. Interestingly, Sparta and Athens were the two cities destined to be the most important of the ancient world.'

'Go on then, tell me about Sparta!'

'Sparta was the most powerful city-state in archaic Greece, and they certainly weren't shy about it. They had a heavily militaristic social system that was very different from that of the other Greek city-states. Legend has it that it was the lawgiver Lycurgus who established this system before calling everyone together to take an oath pledging to observe his laws, even when he happened to be travelling, and not to change anything until he came back. He then left Sparta and disappeared, never to be seen again, so the citizens of Sparta, true to their oath, kept his laws indefinitely.'

'Nothing ever changed?'

'Not until much later. In the Archaic and Classical periods, the Spartans observed Lycurgus's laws. All male citizens received rigorous military training to prepare them for battle, while the women partook in physical exercise just like the men. A Spartan male's allegiance was to the military first and foremost, everything else came in second, and this is what made Sparta a war machine of unparalleled power.'

'Sparta was truly impressive.'

'You really think so? It was a pretty brutal society. Each

year, they held a festival, the Krypteia, during which young Spartan men, under cover of night, were ordered to hunt and kill a slave, also known as a helot. Not to mention the fact that, to varying degrees, Sparta oppressed and intimidated most of the Peloponnese. They fought regularly with Argos and Arcadia, and after subjecting their neighbouring region of Messenia to all manner of misery, they conquered it and turned it into their fiefdom. This was the beginning of a centuries-long enmity between the two cities.'

'Well, there goes the image I had of Sparta!'

'Oh, come on – there's no need to see things as either all black or all white. Sparta is certainly worthy of admiration in some respects, despite its undeniable brutality. I don't know where our need to idealise things comes from. We ought to see things as they are, in the fullness and complexity of both their good and bad sides.'

'But both Sparta and ancient Greece more generally are universally admired.'

'Yes, and for good reason. This does not mean, though, that they were perfect societies. Despite having all of humanity's inevitable weaknesses and flaws, they were societies that succeeded, on a number of different fronts, in producing vital and significant cultures.'

'They also built the great Parthenon!'

'Not yet! The Parthenon was built much later. But since you mention it, it's worth noting that it was during the Archaic period that Greek architecture really began to flourish. Any architectural design that makes you think, "Hmm, that's Greek" – even if it isn't, because the Romans used similar designs later – was created during this period. First came the renowned Doric and Ionic architectural orders. The Doric was adopted mainly by the populations of mainland Greece, most of whom were of Doric descent, and the Ionic mainly by the populations of the islands and Asia Minor, who were mainly of Ionian descent.'

'I can't tell which is which.'

'The Doric is stouter, stockier, with fluted columns with sharp edges topped by a capital – a type of "helmet" at the "head" of the column – that is shaped rather plainly and austerely like a plate or a halved and inverted cone. An ancient temple that embodies the evolution of the Doric order is the Heraion, or Hera's temple, at Olympia. It is one of the most venerable and ancient temples that still remains standing and was originally built with wooden columns that were gradually replaced with stone as they rotted or fell into disrepair. Perhaps because the stone columns were carved in different periods, it turns out that they each represent a different Doric style that varies in proportion and detail. The temple represents the entire Doric gamut, from the early period's shorter and squatter columns with their thicker and rounder capitals that look like little loaves of bread, to the taller and slenderer exemplars of the later period with the plainer, more cone-shaped capitals that we see on the Parthenon.'

'What can you tell me about the Ionic style?'

'The Ionic order was more graceful and maritime in tone. Its fluted columns were slenderer, with the edges of the flutes rounded out, so they weren't razor-sharp like the Doric variety, and the capital came ornamented with two volutes – the quintessential design that comes to mind when anyone, the world over, calls to mind something vaguely resembling "Greek" style. There's also, of course, Aeolia on the northern shores of Asia Minor, where they developed their own style of capital called – wait for it! I bet you'll never guess! – the Aeolic capital, but because it looked quite similar to the Ionic it made neither a big splash nor a lasting impression.'

'Enough with all these columns and capitals! Didn't they make anything else?'

'Oh, this is when Greek art really begins to soar! It hasn't just yet, but you can see it building momentum . . . yes, the culture's creative juices were simmering, on the brink of an eruption in marble and clay. After all, this is the period of the first truly great statues. I've already mentioned that our ancient ancestors liked to travel and were partial to the more advanced civilisations to their east. Egypt, of course, made the greatest impression.'

'Why Egypt?'

'It had an established civilisation that to the Greeks of that time was as ancient as the ancient Greeks are to us today. In Egypt, then, they had a long and fine tradition of building impressive statues in basalt, granite, and other types of such spectacular stone, using the same techniques they'd had since time immemorial. Standing with their arms glued to their sides, the statues had their left leg thrust forward as if trying to keep their balance and not cause a real stir by toppling over onto the first chance passer-by! The Greeks, inspired by this Egyptian model, began to copy it back home.'

'Model?'

'The Egyptians used a canon of proportions for their statues, a set of ideal ratios that ensured the consistency of the human figure. Indeed, according to legend, two Samians, Theodorus and Telecles, sons of Rhoecus – or it may have been Telecles who was the father of the other two, it's all a bit muddled – let's just say, then, that two sculptors from Samos travelled to Egypt to learn the canon of proportions for Egyptian statues. On their return, the two brothers each built half of the statue, split lengthwise from head to toe, in their separate workshops with the goal of melding them together once they were done. Having both closely adhered to the Egyptian measuring system, the two halves fit together perfectly!'

'So in this period, Greeks were making statues that were exact replicas of the Egyptian ones?'

'Not exactly. Although greatly inspired by the Egyptians, the Aegean sculptors built their statues in smaller scale. It was rare to see statues as big as the Egyptians'. This, too, however, did not last long. It was as if the whole thing did not sit well with them.'

'Perhaps they got bored.'

'Or perhaps the style ultimately did not suit their sensibilities and they decided to change things up a bit. First off, while Egyptian statues were always dressed, even if only in a loincloth, the Greeks began to have the males go nude. Then the arms broke free from the figure's sides, and the entire stance became much more natural and less stylised. This was the origin of the type of male statue we know as the kouros, with kore denoting the female version. They also all wore a small, cryptic smile. Besides their naturalistic stance, then, another way to tell if a statue comes from this period is the so-called "archaic smile". This style was first established on the Greek islands, but just like the saying, "if envy were a fever, all the world would be ill", it soon spread and stuck, and we see kouroi appear throughout mainland Greece. Ah, also, I just remembered: legend has it that Theodorus and Rhoecus built an enormous gold krater capable of holding 1,800 litres of wine for Croesus, the King of Lydia!'

'What's a krater?'

'It's a large, two-handled vase used to mix wine and water for the symposia. In other words, the wine would be diluted or mixed (the verb *krási* in ancient Greek), which is where we get the modern Greek noun *krasí* for wine and "krater" for the mixing vessel.'

'No matter what, you always bring me back to pottery!'

'Well, now is the period when the ceramic arts really triumph. The Athenians notice the dark-figure style invented by the Corinthians and they don't skip a beat: if the Corinthians can do it, so can they! As black-figure style's greatest admirers, countless Athenian artists adopt it and produce some of its finest examples. The most eminent are a trio of artists working during the same period in neighbouring workshops located in the narrow, dirty alleys under the Acropolis rock.'

'Tell me about them.'

'Lydos was one of them.'

'Is that a name or his ancestry? Do you mean he came from Lydia?'

'He may have, and that's how he got his name. We also have Exekias and the Amasis Painter.'

'These three were the greatest black-figure style vase painters? Lydos, Exekias, and Amasis?'

'Not Amasis. The Amasis Painter.'

'What's the difference?'

'We don't know his name, but we do know that he painted vases for a potter called Amasis. That's why we call him the Amasis Painter. In fact, Amasis is a foreign, Egyptian name and therefore the man was possibly from Egypt.'

'OK, but you're saying that these characters were the A-listers of vase-painters in Athens at the time?'

'To be precise, of black-figure vase-painters at the time, because shortly before the end of the Archaic period in Athens, we see yet another innovation. In around 530 BCE, a certain potter, Andokides, had a painter in his employ whose name remains unknown.'

'Is he called the Andokides Painter?'

'That's right! You're catching on. This painter, then, appears to have discovered a new trick. Instead of painting the figures black against the clay's orange-red background as per the black-figure style, he decided to switch things around and leave the figures unpainted against a painted black background. Now rendered in the warm red of the lustrous clay, the figures appear more life-like. This new red-figure style soon gained popularity with the many other painters following in the unknown innovator's footsteps.'

'I keep getting the black-figure and the red-figure styles mixed up.'

'It's easy: if the human figures are black, then it's the black-figure style; if they are red, then it's the red-figure style. Some painters used both styles when they decorated vases, with black-figure on one side and red-figure on the other. We call these bilingual vases. See, it's quite the double-entendre of a name, isn't it? We can be quite clever when we want to.'

'Alright, mate, there's no need to make such a song and dance about it. It's hardly the eighth wonder of the world.'

'Enough of your wisecracks! We're talking about the greatest of vase paintings! It's not an accident that Greek vases are among the most important exhibits in museums worldwide. In any case, the first generation of red-figure style ceramics was small, but the following one, the second generation, really pulled out all the stops. These artists begin to fully exploit the possibilities of this new style in representing the human body, and they let their imagination and creativity run wild. They were called the Pioneer Group, not because they discovered the style but because they took it in new and unprecedented directions. They have been described as the first conscious art movement in the history of western art, and it's likely that they were all friends.'

'How do we know that?'

'From their work, and chiefly from the inscriptions on their vases. In fact, what's really amazing is that in addition to other inscriptions, we start to see many of these artists sign their work – a development that allows us to identify them by name: Euphronios, Euthymides, Smikros – probably a nickname due to his small (*mikrós* in Greek) stature – Phintias, Hypsis. Their art also tells us a lot about their personal relationships. A number depict themselves in revelry with their friends. On one such vase, however, we also get a clear signal of competition and possible discord: Euthymides writes that he paints "as never Euphronios could do". At any rate, mired as they were in their personal and creative rivalries and inspirations, I imagine it never occurred to these humble craftsmen that thousands of years later, in the world's largest and most important museums, their work would be studied and hailed as paramount examples of human artistry. No, not even in their wildest dreams, I bet!'

'How did they all end up becoming friends?'

'The Keramikos area of Athens – back then, admittedly, a mere village in size – was the neighbourhood where all the pottery workshops were located. They were manned by artisans: potters, painters, and some who did both. The painters would move from workshop to workshop, while the potters remained stooped over their wheels in narrow rooms full of dirt. Together, they created the vases that today are displayed in the world's greatest museums. Back then, however, people turned up their noses at them. The fact that they did not use their entire bodies but rather sat there, indoors and bereft of sunlight, working with their hands, was thought to be degrading. Yet pottery was lucrative. Attic vases were much in demand throughout the eastern Mediterranean and beyond, along the shores of the Black Sea and even to the west. Potters worked in their mudbrick cabins, leaving the finished products that were for sale either in the front rooms or outside on the street. In the back was the workshop with its potter's wheel and the buckets of dirt, tools hanging from the walls. The potters dressed simply – a tunic and a toga on top for colder days – and were always covered in dirt, their nails permanently red from the clay. After they had been painted, the vessels would dry as they waited their turn for the kiln. It's quite likely that the potters' wives and children would help them with the ceramics.

On the days dedicated to the firing of the vessels, great anxiety prevailed, for this was the most difficult and important phase of their work. They'd stack all the dried vessels into the kiln, light a fire, and feed it to keep it going for the many hours needed to raise the temperature to eight or nine hundred degrees Celsius. If something went wrong during firing, the entire batch might be completely ruined. Weeks of work gone to waste just because the temperature was too high or not high enough, causing the vessels to misfire or worse, crack and shatter. Appeasing the powers that be was therefore a matter of great urgency. They'd gather as many talismans as possible and hang them over the kiln to keep away the malevolent spirits: Syntribos, the great shatterer; Sabaktes, the toppler and destroyer of neat piles; Smaragos, the cracker of vases; Omodamos, the interrupter of the firing process; and Asbetos, the scorcher, who made the fire rage uncontrolled. In fact, both gods and malevolent spirits were always and everywhere present in the lives of the ancient Greeks. Both the symposia and, if you think about it, all the ceramics that we are discussing were dedicated to one god in particular.'

'Dionysus?'

'Yes, my man Dionysus! Perhaps the god who made the greatest impact, because if it weren't for the rituals dedicated to his worship, we would be without half of western culture.'

'Come on! There's no need to exaggerate.'

'I'm not. Dionysus, you know, was a truly unusual god. First, according to legend, he was born twice. The first time was in Boeotian Thebes as the son of Semele, a local princess, who, misled by Hera, asked Zeus to reveal his true self "in all his divine glory" to her.'

'Are you telling me that Semele, even though she was having an affair with Zeus, actually listened to what his wife had to say?'

'Well, yes, the woman was quite gullible! Zeus tried to get her to relent because he knew that her mortal eyes would not withstand the sight, but he had promised to grant her wish, no matter what it was. "Curiosity killed the cat, my dear Semele!" he kept saying, but she insisted, so Zeus did as he had promised: he assumed his true form, all thunder and lightning, engulfing the entire palace in flames and reducing Semele – poor, trusting Semele – to a piece of carbon! Gaia, the Earth goddess, sent tendrils of ivy into the conflagration to entwine themselves around the divine infant and save him. Feeling pity for the little one, Zeus then tore his own thigh open and sewed him in there. This is how, once fully gestated with the divine blood flowing through the father of the gods' leg, Dionysus was born a second time to begin his career as a new god. When you have faced such misadventure from birth and, on top of it all, have a stepmother like Hera hell-bent on making your life difficult, it stands to reason that you're going to have some issues. Indeed, the young Dionysus, in serious need of some R&R, discovered wine. And what does wine call for?'

'What?'

'Revelry. Song and dance. At first, the faithful would sing simple songs in honour of Dionysus that over time evolved into wild choral hymns known as dithyrambs. These songs became Panhellenic hits and were sung at all the festivals and revels. A group of men, in all likelihood dressed as billy goats, would jump up and down as they uttered the lyrics to the songs. This brings us to a certain festival in Attica that I'd like you to picture: the entire village is there, gathered in the fields, either with bottoms planted on the ground or upright on their feet. All is proceeding as usual until a somewhat flighty fellow, Thespis, does something completely out of left field. He goes and stands across from the other singers in the chorus and begins a rudimentary dialogue, a back-and-forth, with them. The chorus issues their choral song and Thespis responds with speech. By introducing the first dialogue into these performances, he becomes the first actor. This, my friend, is the birth of theatre. The moment when, in a mere handful of steps, Thespis assumed his position across from the chorus and opened his mouth to pave the way into the new world of drama, is a moment relived by actors the world over on their opening night when they stride onto the stage. Thespis did not realise what he had given birth to in that moment. He could not have known that for many centuries to come – from the Commedia dell'arte in the Florence of the Medici Renaissance to Shakespeare's Globe on the Queen's Walk along the banks of the Thames, or from Milan's La Scala to New York's Carnegie Hall – he, Thespis, would be the one to kindle the spark in the imaginations of millions of people, an impassioned love of the theatrical arts that would propel many of them to new heights. Where did this spark come from? Perhaps all the way from that palace in Thebes where Dionysus was born.'

'I understand what you're saying, but personally I think ancient Greece gave the world a greater gift than the theatre: democracy! When was democracy established?'

'At around the same time. First off, the kings had to pack up their belongings and clear out, because after everything that had transpired in this period, political change was inevitable. After the overthrow of the monarchy, most Greek states were governed by nobles, members of the aristocracy. Not surprisingly, in some cities the power went to the ruling aristocrats' heads and they abused it by oppressing the less powerful. As a result, and for a variety of different reasons, we see the rise of a new phenomenon in many ancient Greek cities: a certain slick individual – usually an aristocrat, but not necessarily, for the job description called only for plenty of shrewdness, all other qualifications were optional – would ride in as a defender of the oppressed, orchestrate a coup, and take power as a tyrant.'

'You mean a dictator?'

'Back then, the word tyrant did not have such negative connotations. It simply meant someone who had seized power and was governing solo. From Asia Minor and the Aegean Islands to mainland Greece and the Sicilian colonies, then, there were a rising number of smooth operators who, having witnessed the success of the early tyrannies and wishing to keep up with the Joneses, managed to institute tyrannies in their own city-states. Many of them were quite radical; just as many made a point of pandering to their citizenry for obvious reasons: they didn't want to get ousted.'

'Were there many of these tyrants around?'

'Yes, an awful lot. Samos, for example, was governed by a tyrant named Polycrates, who seized power with his two brothers. After initially dividing the island into three, he killed one of them and exiled the other. Lygdamis was the tyrant of Naxos, while Corinth was governed by the tyrant Periander, known, among other things, for kicking his wife to death. He was also a buddy of Thrasybulus, the tyrant of Miletus, to whom Periander had sent a messenger to ask for advice on how best to rule and secure his power. Legend has it that Thrasybulus did not respond; instead, he accompanied the messenger to some fields where he began to cut off the best and tallest ears of wheat. Having heard the message loud and clear, Periander subsequently proceeded to kill any Corinthian whose power and prominence might pose a danger. Sicyon, a small but wealthy city in the northern Peloponnese, was also governed by tyrants. One of them, Cleisthenes, was reputedly the great-grandson of a butcher or a cook, which may have been a fabrication told either to disparage him or, just as easily, to glorify him as a self-made man and not a legacy tyrant. In any case, like in fairy tales, Cleisthenes called the most prominent bachelors in Greece to a competition for the hand of his beloved daughter, Agariste.'

'Why so much detail about Cleisthenes and his family?'

'You'll see why soon enough. Before too long, Sicyon is teeming with suitors, not only from neighbouring city-states but from distant Thessaly and southern Italy. At the end of the competition, two finalists remain, Hippocleides and Megacles, both from Athens, and Cleisthenes, having to choose one, chooses Hippocleides. The wedding festivities are a sight to behold, a hundred cows have been butchered and the entire city and all its luminaries have been invited. Hippocleides, drunk on wine and high spirits, climbs up on a table and starts dancing; indeed, at one point, he stands on his head and kicks his legs up in the air to the beat of the music.'

'Haha! My man was a breakdancer!'

'Yes, an ancient one! Cleisthenes, however, is not impressed. Rather conservative in his tastes, and not expecting such undignified behaviour from his son-in-law, he is, in fact, utterly shocked. Meanwhile, as the groom continues to dance upside down, his entire kit and caboodle, if you know what I mean, is out there on display to all. Angrily, a disgusted Cleisthenes turns to him and declares: "Well done, you've capered and cocked yourself out of a marriage." He wants to make it clear that the dancing and exposed genitalia are more than he can stomach. The drunken Hippocleides responds: "You think I give a damn?" Infuriated, Cleisthenes annuls the marriage and bestows his daughter's hand upon the runner-up, Megacles. This turns out to be a fortunate turn of events for world history, because the new couple names their first son Cleisthenes, after his grandfather, and when Cleisthenes Junior grows to adulthood, he founds democracy in Athens.'

'Did Athens have a tyrant?'

'It did: Peisistratus. He was a shrewd and intelligent man with a flair for drama who assumed power three separate times. In his first attempt, he intentionally wounded himself and his horses, and then went to the city centre and claimed that his life was under threat. On this pretext, he requested and was granted guards for protection from his haters.'

'No one smelled a rat?'

'Only the celebrated Solon, one of the seven wise men of Greece. He had Peisistratus's number and was not shy about shouting it from the rooftops, but no one listened. Peisistratus, in the meantime, had converted his bodyguards into a personal army and seized power. It didn't last long, though, and he was soon exiled. For his second attempt, he dressed up a tall, strapping young woman as the goddess Athena and had her parade all the way from Paeania to Athens in a chariot with him at her side. He wanted to overawe the Athenians with the spectacle of him – the city's rightful ruler – being led back into the city by the patron goddess herself.'

'And Athens fell for the charade again, hook, line, and sinker?'

'Yes, but fortunately not everyone! This time, Peisistratus was driven into exile by Megacles, Cleisthenes's son-in-law I mentioned earlier, of the wealthy and powerful Alcmaeonidae family. Undeterred, Peisistratus returned a third time, after accumulating wealth from mines he owned in Macedonia and with the support of other allied tyrants. The third time was the charm: he seized power and this time it stuck, and he ruled uninterrupted for many years. His opponents, primarily the Alcmaeonidae, went into voluntary exile. Only Solon remained, a lone, loud protester. But he was old, and died soon thereafter.'

'Was Solon not punished for defying the tyrant?'

'No, because he was elderly and venerated. He had cachet. Besides, it's rumoured that he was a former lover of Peisistratus.'

'Really?'

'A number of ancient authors make reference to it. Aristotle is the only one who disputed it due to the great difference in age.'

'After all these attempts, how did Peisistratus manage to remain in power?'

'Peisistratus was a shrewd and successful ruler. He pursued a programme of public works, and also did something that remains popular to this day: he plied the public with spectacle. The pomp and circumstance surrounding the Panathenaic Games and the Dionysia festivals would mark the city's consciousness for the duration of its history. When Peisistratus died, he was succeeded by his sons, Hippias and Hipparchus. At first everything went smoothly, until Hipparchus took a shine to a young man, Harmodius. When Hipparchus made his advances, Harmodius, who happened to already be in a relationship with another man called Aristogeiton, rejected him. In retaliation, Hipparchus publicly insulted Harmodius's little sister, saying that she was lying about being a virgin and was therefore unfit to take part in Athens' public festival.'

'Was virginity that important?'

'Of course. The insult was terrible, and only maidens were allowed to take part in the parade for the goddess Athena. Therefore, on the day of the festival, Harmodius and his lover, Aristogeiton, lay in wait and stabbed the tyrant Hipparchus. Later, they would be honoured as Tyrannicides and leaders in the cause of Athenian democracy. After his brother's death, Hippias, now left to his own devices, went a little mad and became much more brutal and despotic, so much so that after some time the Athenians, requesting intervention from Sparta, revolted and sent him into exile. It was at that time of social turmoil that the younger Cleisthenes I mentioned earlier suddenly popped up, in the year 508 BCE, and suggested something truly radical: democracy. After seeing the establishment of city-states, the dissemination of writing, and the planting of the seeds that would flower into high art, architecture, philosophy, theatre, and the branches of knowledge, the Archaic period was coming to a close. Still a newborn at the time, democracy was destined to struggle for its survival. A trial by fire was not long in putting in an appearance, for a large and almighty empire, Persia, was sharpening her claws, eyes fixed belligerently on this part of the world.'

'OK – a break, please, for a question!'

'What question?'

'All this time you've been bombarding me with words I don't know. I'm drowning under all the jargon! What is it with you scholarly types and all the highfalutin vocabulary?'

FAQ

No More Difficult Words, I Promise!
Why So Much Jargon?

'I COMPLETELY UNDERSTAND why you find it confusing, daunting, dreary. You're right: jargon can be tedious and difficult to understand. But it also has a purpose, a *raison d'être*. When a discipline involves thousands of people from around the world, we need a common vocabulary, an agreement about naming conventions, in order to communicate.'

'Can't you just say, "we've found a vessel"? Do you really need five hundred different words for it?'

'What kind of vessel, though? They're all vessels! We need

a way to tell them apart, don't we? No matter what, precise terminology is critical to a discipline. That said, though, I acknowledge that there's probably no urgent need for it outside the confines of scholarly publication and discussion, or analyses and disagreements among experts in the field. It stands to reason, also, that with the passage of time, terminology changes: new terms and meanings will be added, while old ones will be withdrawn or go defunct.'

'The problem with jargon is that it always comes out, and often takes over, whenever the discipline attempts to communicate with the rest of the world. It's just not helpful. Isn't clear communication what you scholars aim for?'

'You are right about that. The rest of the world does not need to know all the ins-and-outs of disciplinary terminology. Obviously, in the time we have, I cannot discuss the issue of terminology as a whole, nor can I offer definitions for each term used in the discipline. That said, I also need to point out that I didn't bombard you with jargon. Not by a long shot! I haven't even scratched the surface of disciplinary jargon. And let me tell you, there are plenty of examples of odd, inconsistent, or even absurd terminology that "speaks" only to an archaeologist and no one else.'

'Now I'm curious. Give me some examples.'

'The alabastron of the Mycenaean period is a squat, circular jar that resembles a small, round loaf of bread and was probably used to store unguents and cosmetics (fig. 1 on page 150). The alabastron of classical antiquity, however, is completely different. This alabastron, a narrow vessel that resembles the volumetric flasks found in chemistry labs, was used to store perfumes and essential oils (fig. 2). The exaleiptron is a rather odd, squat, and rounded vessel from classical antiquity, similar to the Mycenaean alabastra I just mentioned, but with a deep, overhanging, and inward-turning lip that prevents spillage (fig. 3). At one time, we called them kothones, but now that name is no longer in use. When the exaleiptron comes with a foot, we call it a plemochoe (fig. 4). Don't ask me why – just because. There are also deep drinking cups with two horizontal handles positioned at the rim that are called skyphoi (fig. 5). There are dozens of different types of skyphoi. One type is called the bolsal skyphos (fig. 6), because when the first two exemplars were examined many years ago, one was located in Bologna, Italy, and the other in Thessaloniki or Salonica. Ergo, Bol-ogna and Sal-onica give us Bolsal. Another type of skyphos is called a CHC (fig. 7), because they are often decorated with images of either chariots or scenes of courtship. Ch-ariots and C-ourtship give us CHC. Also, the skyphos and the kotyle are basically the same type of vessel.'

'Well, there you go! None of it makes any sense.'

'Wait, slow down, it gets worse. Let's turn to the glossary of weapons terminology. Take a shield: it's never referred to simply as a shield (fig. 8), but as a hoplon or an aspis. The metal straps on the inside that provide a solid grip and serve as an armrest of sorts are not called grips, they are the porpax. The shield's metal rim is not called a metal rim, it's the itys. Then we get to helmets, and we're deep in your favourite thing, a rat's nest! The Illyrian helmet wasn't actually from Illyria (fig. 9).'

'What do you mean by Illyrian?'

'The Illyrians were a people who lived in what we'd call north-western Greece and south-eastern Albania today. The Illyrian helmet, however, is in fact Greek, and originally hailed from southern Greece before becoming popular throughout the rest of the country. What happened is that because the first

such helmets were discovered in the region of ancient Illyria, the name stuck. Corinthian helmets, though, have been called that since antiquity (fig. 10). In fact, Herodotus, in describing the ancient tribes of Libya, the Machlyes and the Auseans, mentions their custom of dressing a young woman in armour and a Corinthian helmet, and having her parade around a lake in a chariot. This procession would open the ritual battle between two armies of young women in which the casualties were said to have lied about their virginity.'

'What? That's pretty random!'

'True. But the story is so surreal, I had to share it with you.'

'To confuse me even more! Tell me more about the helmets.'

'The Corinthian helmet is the most well-known today. In fact, it has become the archetypal ancient Greek helmet, you see it in all the movies and souvenir shops – even Magneto in Marvel Comics' *X-Men* wears one. The Chalcidian helmet, generally considered an adaptation of the Corinthian variety, was named by researchers who saw it depicted on vases which they believed hailed from Chalkida, even though there is absolutely no evidence for this. The Boeotian helmet has been called that since antiquity (fig. 11). Xenophon refers to it and suggests that it is most suitable for charioteers or horsemen. What today we call the Attic helmet, on the other hand, never became very famous (fig. 12), but the Romans copied it and made one of its adaptations a real hit. It's the one you see every Roman soldier wearing.'

'I know I keep repeating this, but you're frying my brain.'

'But we're not even close to being done! Shall we return to pottery? There is a category of ancient vessel that we call Melian, because they were first found on the island of Milos.

But we now know that they were from Paros. Just like a very special kind of vessel, made out of exceptionally clean and fine clay as delicate as crystal, that we used to call Naucratic, because they were first found in Naucratis in Egypt, a Panhellenic trading post and colony that had been given to the Greeks by the Pharaohs. Now, though, we called them Chiote because we discovered that they were actually made in Chios (fig. 13).'

'OK, so in this instance, you ditched the old terminology and updated it – it's enough to drive you mad!'

'I'm not finished yet! In late antiquity, there were small vessels used to store myrrh and other essential oils that were called myrrodochoeia. They're found in almost every tomb from the Hellenistic period onwards. We used to call these vessels tear-catchers.'

'Why? Because they held the tears shed by those mourning their dead?'

'For some time, we also used a term that was translated from the Latin, since these types of vessels were also very popular in the Roman period, and they were called lacrimataria. We now call them unguentaria.'

'Good grief!'

'Kyathos is what we call the ladle used since the Classical period to spoon wine from the krater into a cup, which is not called a cup, but a kylix, or skyphos, or kotyle, or . . . what have you. On the other hand, ethmos is what we call the strainer, because it was customary to soak various herbs and aromatics in the wine for flavour, so it had to be strained before drinking. We use the word peronai for the pins they used to hold their garments together, and then we also have the klismos chair, the peplos or the chiton for various types of tunic and . . . right! I'm done!'

'Yes, I've had enough too! But I think you archaeologists owe an apology to every museumgoer who has fled from an exhibition because of all the gibberish on the captions.'

'Oh, stop complaining! Let's move on, because the best is yet to come.'

'What do you mean?'

'Does the sentence "This is Sparta!" mean anything to you?'

8

Another One Bites The Dust
(The Greco-Persian Wars)

'ONCE UPON A TIME, an empire was born in Mesopotamia, a region of the world not unfamiliar with empires over the many centuries of its existence. The Medes and the Persians were related peoples who collaborated on the founding of this particular empire, and it grew to be the greatest the world had seen at the time.'

'Oh, no! You're taking me all the way back . . . Can't we just get to the action?'

'Didn't I tell you to stop complaining? We'll get to the action soon enough. If you don't know anything about whom the Greeks fought in the Greco-Persian wars, how can you possibly understand why their win was so important?'

'Oh, please, why all the drama? It's simple: the Persian Empire was brutal and uncivilised; their only goal was conquest.'

'You really think that's all there was to it? Obviously, it was a harsh society that was eager for conquest, like all empires before and after, but, at the same time, in order to create such an expansive and complex state, it had to have both a good infrastructure and technical know-how. It succeeded in uniting hundreds of different states under its power by allowing them religious freedom. The arts were supported, and flourished. Persia very quickly grew into a superpower that subjugated Egypt, all the Middle East, and even Asia Minor. Even though Greek regions in Asia Minor were located mainly along the coast, they too succumbed to the indomitable Persian tidal wave. At some point, however, the Greek states rebelled. They sent a message to their brethren on the Greek mainland to come to their aid.'

'Wait a sec, didn't the Persian Wars take place in Greece?'

'You're getting ahead of yourself. We're not yet at the wars. What I'm talking about is the Ionian Revolt. So, where was I? Ah, yes: most of the Greeks on the mainland either chickened out or didn't want to help. Two city-states were exceptions: Eretria and Athens. They sent troops to help fight the Persian bully. As you can probably guess, the Ionian Revolt of 492 BCE failed, and the Greek cities of Asia Minor now found themselves definitively under the Persian yoke. The Persians, who were definitely not born yesterday, noted the role the Athenians and the Eretrians had played and decided to punish them as an example – after all, they couldn't have these Greek states threatening their stability. This, my friend, was the beginning of the First Persian War. In 490 BCE, two years after the revolt, Persia sends its troops to Eretria. They besiege the city and burn it to the ground – pure massacre and destruction! From there, they set sail for Attica, just across the narrow Gulf. The Persian fleet lands at the Bay of Marathon and an army the likes of which Greece has never seen begins to pile out.'

'The Greeks didn't unite against the Persians?'

'Not at that point. The Athenians send out an SOS. They dispatch a messenger, Pheidippides, to Sparta to request help, and he runs there and back, covering more than two hundred kilometres in a few days. It turns out that his exertions are for naught, though, because the superstitious Spartans, wary of the full moon as a bad omen, want to wait for it to pass before sending their army out of the city.'

'So all that running and nothing came of it?'

'According to legend, somewhere in the middle of the route, on the slopes of Mount Parthenion, Pheidippides stopped among the kermes oaks to catch his breath. That's when a miracle occurred: a minor god decided to help the Athenians. The story is that the god Pan appeared before Pheidippides and declared that he would stand by the Athenians if they agreed to worship him. Pheidippides promised to relay the god's message to them upon his arrival, which is exactly what he did, and instead of suspecting that all the running had gone to the poor fellow's head, the Athenians actually believed him, and vowed to worship Pan.'

'But they received no help?'

'Neither from the Spartans nor from most other Greeks. Only the Plataeans managed to send some troops, but they were small in number, about one thousand men all in all. You realise, don't you, that Athens was in very real danger of complete catastrophe? All eligible citizens of this small city that only a few years earlier had adopted democracy and taken its fate into its own hands were called to take arms and prove to the world that democracy works, that a village on the edge of the world is capable of defying the bellicose monster of empire! The young soldiers gathering at Marathon to face the Persian hordes could see the smoke billowing from the razing of Eretria across the way, and they knew that their turn had come. The Athenians had about nine or ten thousand hoplites, but they were confronting an army of many times that number.'

'How much bigger was it?'

'Between two to ten times that number – it's unclear, and estimates abound. In any case, the Athenians came up with an ingenious strategy: they left the centre of their formation sparsely populated while fortifying their flanks. As a result, when the lines made contact and the Greek centre began to retreat in response to the enemy onslaught, the Greek flanking troops prevailed in the wings, and before long they had turned inward, like pincers, and surrounded the Persian centre on both sides. At the critical moment, the pincer closed, and it was game over for the stunned Persians! No wonder, then, that legend has it that it was Pan who, gratified by the Athenians' devotion, had lent a helping hand by spreading fear among the Persians – a fear named after him. The Persians panicked. Two hundred and three Greek casualties, as opposed to around six thousand five hundred on the Persian side.'

'So the word panic comes from the god Pan? That never occurred to me.'

'The Persians then break in disarray, fleeing to their ships with the Athenians in pursuit. According to legend, a certain Cynaegirus on the Athenian side literally holds onto the prow of a Persian ship to prevent it from leaving! Panic-stricken, the Persians cut off his hand. Undeterred, Cynaegirus grabs the prow with his other hand and the Persians cut that off too. Cynaegirus then sinks his teeth into the prow, and off comes his head! As they set sail, it occurs to the Persians that with the entire Athenian army gathered at Marathon, far from home base, the city has been left entirely unprotected. "It's ripe for the taking!" they think to themselves as they steer toward Phaleron, the city's harbour. The Athenian troops, however, are no dummies: they know what the Persians are thinking.

Despite their exhaustion, they dash back to the city as fast as they can.'

'Seriously? How could they, exhausted as they were and wearing all that heavy armour?'

'That's what's so impressive about it! Those young hoplites, completely debilitated after hard battle with a mighty foe, left their wounded behind and began racing down the gruelling road of return from Marathon to Athens to save their small city. In fact, they did an entire marathon clad in full armour!'

'Did they make it back in time?'

'They did. When the Persian fleet arrived in Phaleron, it was greeted by the sight of the Athenian troops proudly lining the hills outside the city, shields and spears glittering under the sun. It didn't take long for the Persians to realise that the game was up; they turned tail and returned home. That was the end of the First Persian War that saw the destruction of Eretria and the triumph of Athens. Not surprisingly, the Battle of Marathon became legendary, and following generations built entire myths around it, weaving in stories about gods, like Pan, who had reputedly lent a helping hand, or even Theseus himself, the mythical hero and legendary founder of Athens in the distant past, who is said to have dropped in at the battle . . . This is a line of thinking that we also see in more recent generations, when they claim that the Virgin Mary, or certain saints and divinities, are fighting on their side on the battlefield. For Persia, however, the insult of defeat rankled. It spent ten years gathering and preparing an army in order to launch a long-awaited sequel, the Second Persian War, in 480 BCE.'

'Once again by sea?'

'No. This time the Persians travel by land and bring a much larger army. They are accompanied by an enormous fleet, but on this occasion, it is the infantry that is truly something to behold. They conquer Thrace, subjugate Macedonia, and are beginning to believe – not without reason, of course – that the rest will fall like dominoes and that the entire Greek peninsula will soon be inducted into the social patchwork of their empire. In the meantime, though, the King of Macedon, Alexander I, despite appearing to cooperate with Persia, is secretly relaying information to the Greeks of the south. Quite a few Greek cities, fearing for their fates, fall all over themselves to declare their surrender. This includes the Delphi priesthood, who prefer a safe bet on the predicted victor than to put themselves at risk.'

'You mean that the ancient world's foremost oracle predicts the invaders' victory?'

'Yes, but most Greek cities ignore it and present a united front against the foreign threat. The Spartans, the greatest power in Greece at the time, take the lead. The first line of defence is at Thermopylae – a fly could not have squeezed through! But treason forces the Greeks to retreat. Athens, despite its resounding victory ten years earlier, is now abandoned and falls to the Persians, who raze it to the ground. Carrying everything they are able to, the Athenians flee and seek refuge in nearby islands. Only the Peloponnese is still free, and at the Panhellenic Military Council they discuss staunching the Persian advance at the Isthmus.'

'I'm nervous. Why am I nervous? I know that it all ends well.'

'The Athenian general, Themistocles, observing the lay of the land and aware that the Greek forces have their greatest advantage at sea, challenges the Persian fleet to a battle in the Straits of Salamis. The Greek fleet storms and rages in their triremes. The sailors manning them are not superheroes; they are simply young men who, having witnessed their relatives' frantic flight with the foe snapping at their heels and their city consumed in flames, know they have nothing left. They either fight for the win or lose everything. And guess what? They win! The Greeks, with the Athenian fleet stealing the spotlight, emerge as victors in the naval Battle of Salamis because the smaller Greek ships are better able to manoeuvre in the melee than their cumbersome Persian counterparts. The Persian emperor Xerxes, perched in his crow's nest on Mount Aigaleo overlooking the straits of Salamis, observes the entire naval battle unfold before his eyes, probably choking on his arrogance all the while.'

'Yes, but it was one victory at sea. Was that enough?'

'The battle at sea helps the Greeks gain time, and the Persians, now without a navy, cannot get supplies to their troops. Having had time to rally, the Greek ground forces are able to vanquish the Persians at the Battle of Plataea. Now thoroughly beaten, the Persians make a hasty retreat. Greek ships follow them to Mycale on the shores of Asia Minor, where they trounce them yet again.'

'Like a final slap in the bully's face.'

'After taking some time to lick its wounds and clear the ashes left behind by the wars, Greece was ready to take the next big step up with a new self-image and a reinvigorated sense of its power. On the brink of the Classical period, it was time for Greece to truly shine! So let's talk about what transpired during the Classical period that marks it as one of the most important periods in world history.'

'Wait! Before you tell me about that . . . I have a question. You said that Athens was burned down to the ground, and I thought of something that I have always wondered about and have never understood. Why are these ancient cities always buried deep underground? How is that possible?'

FAQ

How Do Cities and Antiquities End Up So Deep Underground?

'THIS IS PROBABLY the most common question I come across. The answer is quite simple: it's because people continue to live in the same location for many centuries.'

'I still don't understand.'

'Alright, here we go, with more detail: first, the earth's crust is not stable; soil and dirt are constantly on the move. The crust is a textured layer comprised of different materials, basically stones and dirt. In some areas of the globe, it gathers over mountains; in others, it stretches over plains. There is also water, and plenty of it, found either in the seas, or – and this is of greater concern to us – in rivers and lakes. Obviously, this water, too, is constantly on the move, repurposing itself. There are rains; icefalls, landslips and rockslides of all varieties; rivers that carry sediment, change their course, abandon their deltas, and carve new paths through the earth. There are also earthquakes, volcanic eruptions, tidal bores – utter chaos, I tell you! Our landscape, the ground beneath our feet, is constantly changing. The layers of earth that collect or build over centuries are called strata.'

'Are strata the same everywhere?'

'No. They can vary in thickness from a few centimetres to several metres. Now add the imponderable and extremely critical variable called the human being into the equation. Humans obviously flock to hospitable locations, usually flatlands or gently rolling hills, often located near water. Generally, they do not prefer steep and rocky mountainous regions, nor do they aspire to reach for the skies at the ends of the earth. Humans favour accessible terrain, and wherever they choose to settle, they dig, they plough, they remove or add soil. In short, they're constantly working with and moving dirt, and most of all, they build. For thousands of years, human construction involved the layering of organic material on organic material: wood, brick, stone. The earth, the materials offered by the surrounding landscape – that's what they used to satisfy their needs. Humans, however, are also careless, trigger-happy, at the mercy of the whims of chance. An oil lamp topples to the ground, an unattended pot sparks, and whoosh, you have a fire; not to mention earthquakes or enemy incursions ... in general, there are thousands of ways that a house, a neighbourhood, an entire city can be razed to the ground. Even when they're not destroyed in their entirety, they get old, they fall into ruin, and the only thing to do is to level and rebuild.'

'Don't you need to dig deep, though, for the foundations?'

'First of all, foundations back in the day weren't as deep as the ones needed for today's enormous buildings. Second, have you by chance been to an archaeological site and observed such a hotchpotch of ruined walls that you find it almost impossible to make sense of the building layout?'

'Yup.'

'Well, that's because you are seeing different stages of construction all at once. In the meantime, rains and the movement of soil, either by natural or human forces, painfully slowly and mostly unintentionally, begin to add height to the soil layer. All this activity is what creates these so-called strata. It stands to reason, then, that in Greece, where most cities have been inhabited for several thousands of years, we see the accumulation of various strata. Even ancient cities that have since remained uninhabited exhibit this layering of strata.'

'Are these strata always very deep?'

'There's great variation. Let's take Ancient Olynthus as an example. Razed to the ground in classical antiquity and located on two flat-topped hills that hindered the accumulation of large quantities of soil, its strata are very different from those found at the site of Ancient Messene. The latter, built in a valley at the foot of a mountain that funnelled both water and soil onto it for several thousands of years, is remarkable for the thick strata that kept its ruins exceptionally well-preserved. What we see, then, is that some ancient cities are buried under tons of earth; others under much less; and still others, like the Acropolis, remain completely untouched.'

'Why wasn't the Acropolis, or sites like it, ever covered?'

'Because they were always in use. The Athenian Acropolis was never deserted. Indeed, after the fifth century BCE, it has never been completely destroyed and rebuilt.'

'But why was it destroyed and rebuilt in the fifth century?'

'Well, as I mentioned a little while ago, it was burned and destroyed by the Persians when they invaded Athens in 480 BCE. Fifty years later, it was rebuilt from scratch – and beautifully, I might add. Indeed, to this day it remains the pre-eminent symbol of classical Greece, among other things.'

'Phew! So we are finally in the Classical period?'

'Oh, yes, my friend.'

'It's about time!'

9

Glory Days
(The Classical Period)

'THAT'S IT, we're finally at the era you've been waiting for.'

'The crowning moment of ancient Greek civilisation, correct?'

'Well, I wouldn't call it a moment! It lasted approximately one hundred and fifty years, but there is general agreement that it represents the pinnacle of ancient Greek culture.'

'Why?'

'Because the achievements of this period have struck scholars throughout the ages – as much then as now – as unparalleled. Not without reason, I would add.'

'You mean that cultural developments before and after this period were not as impressive?'

'No, on the contrary – as we've already discussed, much of what we admire about antiquity has already occurred, and much of it would continue to evolve after the Classical period. It's just that in this period we see the development of a critical mass of cultural production that is directly responsible for the general perception of ancient Greece as a unique force in the history of the world.'

'Good grief! That sounds both vague and pretentious. Could you be a little more specific?'

'You're right. OK, here goes: Classical Greece is flanked by two momentous events: the Persian Wars, and the life and times of Alexander the Great. In other words, the Classical period extends from 480 BCE, when the Persian Wars come to an end, to the death, in 323 BCE, of Alexander the Great. He blazed a trail that changed the entire world, and his death therefore serves as a fitting marker to the end of the Classical period.'

'So what happened in that period?'

'First, having vanquished the world's greatest empire at the time, the Greeks rise from the ashes sporting a new self-image and a whole new sense of confidence. The pride in their triumph serves as a general fillip, like a bracing vitamin shot that strengthens all aspects of society.'

'Was Sparta still supreme among Greek city-states?'

'Yes, in a certain sense, but Athens's star was rising, and, wreathed in the aura of having dealt the definitive blow in the victory against the Persians, it gradually took centre stage. It built alliances with many other cities, especially on the islands, and formed a confederacy against the Persians.'

'But hadn't they already defeated Persia?'

'They had, but Persia still posed a danger. The Greeks knew that they couldn't just rest on their laurels, that they had to be prepared for any eventuality. With the small island of Delos, Apollo's sacred island, designated as their central meeting place, the coalition was named the Delian League. But since the entire League was ruled almost single-handedly by Athens, it is sometimes referred to as the Athenian League or the Athenian Empire. At some point, the League's coffers were transferred from Delos to Athens with the excuse that Delos was small and vulnerable and the money needed to be protected. At the time, you see, there was no safer place than the Acropolis of Athens. But to be honest, Athens does not appear to have been all that great of an ally to its comrades in arms. In fact, it bled them dry.'

'What do you mean?'

'I mean that for many cities and islands, the League's levies – their membership dues, in other words – were extortionate, and if a city wanted to withdraw . . . well, they simply weren't allowed to. Athenian troops would sweep in and with the sheer force of their military power compel the unwilling party to remain. In general, they ran roughshod over the entire Aegean.'

'That doesn't make classical Athens look all that good. Is our image of it wrong?'

'Not exactly. Perhaps it's rather one-sided. I've said it before: nothing is just black or white. Classical Athens was many things at once, and despite – or perhaps because of – this complexity, we mustn't forget that classical Athens was a most impressive city indeed.'

'When was the Golden Age of Pericles?'

'At this same time. As Athens ascends to the pinnacle of its power and glory, Pericles from Cholargos, the charismatic politician who went down in history, is the one steering the ship. His mother, Agariste, was a scion of the Alcmaeonidae. You remember them?'

'The rich and powerful noble family that exiled the Athenian tyrants?'

'Yes. According to legend, when Agariste was pregnant, she dreamt that she gave birth to a lion. You see what this legend is trying to convey, don't you?'

'Did she really dream that?'

'Oh, come on, are you serious? Rulers would often disseminate stories like this one to create more of a buzz or mystique around their personas. In Pericles's case, of course, the joke was on him, because the dream was interpreted as a reference to his disfigurement. He is reputed to have been born with a disfigured skull, which is why in all the busts we have of him, he appears wearing a helmet pushed back on his head to camouflage its shape. In any case, Pericles was a political genius, who had a long-term romantic relationship with a courtesan, or hetaira, named Aspasia. She was an educated and brilliant woman who wielded great political influence over him.'

'OK, but . . . a courtesan? You mean a prostitute?'

'A hetaira was not a prostitute in the way we understand the word today. They were educated single women who refused to lead conventional married lives. Interestingly and paradoxically, even though they clearly strayed from the norms of the time, they were often both welcomed and celebrated among powerful and educated male circles. Since they had no other way to make a living, they charged for their services, both intellectual and sexual.'

'I've heard of Aspasia of Miletus, but she's the only famous courtesan I know of.'

'There's also Phryne, whose life was like a movie. She was born in a remote Boeotian village, but as soon as she was able to, she packed her few belongings and headed out to chance her luck in the big city of Athens. She reputedly charged exorbitant amounts for her sexual services – one night was equivalent to a hundred day's wages – and the less she liked someone, the more she charged. She made an exception, however, for the eccentric and penniless philosopher Diogenes. (He voluntarily slept in a large ceramic jar. Need I say more?) To him, she offered herself for free, because she found his mind utterly fascinating.'

'She was a beautiful woman, eh?'

'Oh, she was that alright – as beautiful as they come. Once, while attending one of the seaside festivals, she found herself sweltering from the heat so she threw off her clothes and dove naked into the water in front of everyone, including the painter Apelles of Kos, who was inspired by the sight to paint *Aphrodite Anadyomene*, or *Venus Rising from the Sea*. Similarly, the sculptor Praxiteles, with whom she had a relationship, created the first nude female statue of antiquity, the *Aphrodite of Cnidus*, in her image. Even though the statue provoked outrage, it became an instant classic. Phryne herself was dragged through the Athenian courts on the charge of being a bad influence on young women. According to legend, during the trial, her lawyer pulled off her tunic to reveal her nakedness. She was so beautiful that the dumbfounded jurors immediately acquitted her. In another version of the story, Phryne deliberately shook each juror's hand before asking them to acquit her. And guess what? They did.'

'You mean all she had to do was touch them?'

'One touch was enough. She was Aphrodite, after all.'

'It looks like our ancient ancestors had a real soft spot for beauty.' He smiled slyly.

'They were also quite superstitious. While beauty was deemed a favour from the gods, ugliness was seen as punishment. A tad unjust, don't you think? And come to think of it, that's the least of it. They had some truly crazy superstitions. A good case in point is the surreal sacrificial ceremony called the Buphonia, during which they would sacrifice an ox on the highest point of the Acropolis. Due to their central role in agricultural production, however, it was prohibited to sacrifice oxen – they were essential to the cultivation of the earth and human subsistence. What they'd do to get around this prohibition, then, was place some grain on the altar, drive the oxen towards it, and the first ox to eat of the grain was seen as having self-selected for sacrifice by committing the offense of "stealing" the divinities' offering! Despite the beast's guilt, its actual killing was strictly not a public spectacle. Everyone would file out as cool as a cucumber, pretending they had no idea what was about to happen, leaving behind a single priest armed with an axe. After slaying the ox, the priest would immediately drop the axe and flee the scene, so that when the others returned, they'd be treated to the spectacle of the poor dead ox, but no sign of his killer. The only clue was the axe, still in the same spot where it had been dropped. So what would our good ancestors do? They would blame the axe for the killing! No harm, no foul.'

'That's completely mad! What a performance. Who were they kidding? They knew exactly what was going on.'

'I told you! Not what you expected from the birthplace of democracy, is it? A place eulogised by none other than the great Bob Dylan himself in his Nobel speech: "All that culture from a thousand years ago, that philosophy, that wisdom – Plato, Aristotle, Socrates – what happened to it?" But no, my friend, our ancient ancestors were superstitious sorts who believed that inanimate objects possessed agency, volition, and could therefore be punished. Next time you give your printer a good punch because it's giving you a hard time and all the paper has jammed or whatnot, just know that you're letting out your inner ancient Greek.'

'So that's what they were doing up there on the Acropolis, the "pinnacle of ancient Greek culture"!'

'Not so fast, my friend! It remains an important symbol and is truly mind-blowing as a monument. The Acropolis is recognised as the finest achievement of Greek sculpture and architecture.'

'Why?'

'Well, with coffers full of Delian League funds, Athens thought it was high time to make herself look spectacular. Pericles launched the most ambitious building programme in Greek history, with temples going up throughout Attica, including Sounion, Eleusis, the Temple of Hephaestus in the ancient Agora, and so on. In fact, Attica became one big construction site. The renovation and rebuilding of the Acropolis was the cornerstone of the programme. This is where the insuperable Parthenon, a building that is probably closer to perfection than any other, was built.'

'Why is the Parthenon superior to other ancient temples?'

'There are many reasons. First of all, the entire thing is built in marble – even the tiles. And we're not talking some inferior quality marble, we're talking Pentelic marble, the prime, fine-grained stuff that shimmers like a symphony in stone for the eye.'

'Yeah, but how good is it really? A few years ago, I took some relatives who were visiting from Australia to see it, and I was struck by the fact that it isn't white any more. How good can it be if it has turned pink over time? Why didn't it stay white?'

'Pentelic marble contains particles of iron, which is why it has that faintly rosy glow that renders its overall effect even warmer and sweeter. The Temple of Poseidon at Sounion, for example, was built with an Agrileza marble that does not contain iron and is still snow-white. Of course, in that location, the sharp contrast of the white marble against the blue of the Aegean is truly stunning.'

'You're wandering, mate! How did we get to Sounion? You were telling me about the Acropolis.'

'That's right. Let's continue. Second, the Parthenon, instead of the customary six columns on the façade and back – in other words, the narrower sides of the building – has eight. Correspondingly, instead of the customary fifteen columns on the wider sides, it has seventeen. This made it larger and more imposing than the typical Greek temple.'

'All these numbers. Are they supposed to impress me?'

'Alright, then, my friend, here's something that I think will impress: ancient craftsmen were aware that Pentelic marble possesses a strange quality that can be described as a "sponginess" or "spread" – in other words, after excavation, the stone dilates for a few years – so they left tiny gaps between each marble slab. Over time, once the pieces of stone had expanded to their definitive size, they closed the gap and formed an airtight seal. When contemporary renovations required the prying apart of pieces of column that had not been disturbed since antiquity, the air was filled with the scent of the now-exposed connecting wooden joints!'

'Wow!'

'There's more. Third: the Parthenon was the only temple to be so lavishly decorated at the time. Every single one of its metopes was carved with sculptural decoration.'

'What's a metope?'

'You know how temples have a long horizontal lintel that rests on the columns? Have you noticed how, directly over each column, there's a rectangular channelled tablet consisting of three vertical bands?' I took my phone, googled 'ancient Greek temple' and showed him what I meant.

'I see . . .'

'Those are the triglyphs. Originally, this is where the notched ends of the wooden beams that held up the roof on the earliest wooden temples were located. When they began building temples out of marble, they kept this representation of the beam-end design as a decorative element.'

'But what about the metopes?'

'I'm getting to them. Metopes are the rectangular, recessed spaces between the triglyphs. Instead of having them gawp there empty, they were covered in decorative carvings, for they provided nice open spaces that could easily accommodate a sculpture and tell a story. And the Parthenon does not lack for metopes – ninety-two in total! Each one is stunning and brimming with symbolism.'

'What do they symbolise?'

'On the east side of the building, over the main entrance, the metopes depict the Gigantomachy, the battle against the Giants, or, to be more exact, the Olympian gods' victory over the primitive powers at the beginning of the world and time. It's an allegory for the victory of the new gods of order and divine power over deities that symbolised primordial chaos. The metopes on the south side depict the Centauromachy, the battle between humans and centaurs, or human victory over primordial monsters. It could also be interpreted as the victory of human civilisation and refinement over the wilder, more savage parts of their nature. The metopes on the north side depict the Trojan War, the most renowned epic of the triumph in battle by Greece's heroic ancestors; while the metopes of the west side tell the story of the Amazonomachy, in which the

Amazons set off from Asia to conquer Athens and are defeated under the Acropolis. You see, don't you, how this story resonates loudly with the Athenian experience at the time? The builders of the Parthenon had grandparents who had survived such an attack and had successfully defended themselves against the Persian threat.'

'These are the most important Parthenon sculptures?'

'No, those are only the metopes. The temple has many more and much more important sculptures, like those found on its pediments.'

'What now is a pediment?' He huffed.

'A pediment is the triangular space between the uppermost horizontal beam and the roof found at the façade and back of every temple. Given that the east side of the temple housed the main entrance and therefore its most sacred façade, the east pediment depicts Athena's birth as she springs forth from Zeus's head. The west pediment depicts Athena's contest with Poseidon for dominion over Athens. The statues were all exquisitely sculpted in the round, in other words they can be viewed from any angle, and the same care was lavished on both the front and back, even though the latter could not be seen once the sculptures were placed in position in their high pediments. Sadly, they were all greatly damaged over the years, and many are no longer in Greece, even though the Greek government has formally requested their return.'

'Why all this to-do over the Parthenon Marbles?'

'Because they were created at a time when sculpture was truly branching out and breaking free of the Archaic mould; not to mention the fact that they were the work of none other than the renowned sculptor Phidias. We also mustn't forget the large and stunningly beautiful frieze, the horizontal band that runs the length of the upper inner wall of the temple, depicting the Panathenaic procession and replete with a great variety of exceptionally carved figures. The odd thing is that the frieze is typical of the Ionic order of temple, not the Doric. Yet the Parthenon, a Doric temple, has a frieze – don't ask me why, just because! Another innovation. Besides, every single figure on the metopes, the pediments, and the frieze is different. And that's not all.'

'There's more?'

'Yes, my friend, there is! All the Parthenon's proportions adhere to the golden 4:9 ratio. We see it in the relation of its overall width to its overall length, the height of the façade to its width, and so on and so forth. What's more, there are no straight lines in the Parthenon. In fact, they appear straight because they all have a very slight convex curve. This is due to a phenomenon called entasis that was meant to counteract an optical effect in which rectilinear columns appear to be slenderer in the middle. The Parthenon's optical effects were calculated with surgical precision.'

'It must have taken them many years to do such meticulous and detailed work.'

'Well, you're touching on another impressive fact about the Acropolis: It was built in nine years. Throw in the other six that it took them to complete all the finishing decorative details and it's a total of fifteen years for the building of one of the world's premier cultural monuments. A product of tireless work not only by Athenians of every stripe and craft specialisation, but also by the Greeks from every corner of the land who had flocked to Athens as migrants, both enslaved and free, all of them paid the same daily wage. Indeed, even the beasts of burden were essential to the completion of the project. There's a tale about an elderly donkey that beautifully illustrates this point. Judged unable to continue bearing all that weight up and down the Acropolis, an attempt was made to put the poor thing out to grass, but the creature refused to stop working. Onlookers watched it climbing up the rock of its own accord, next to the younger donkeys carrying heavy loads, as if to guide the novices and show them how it's done. The Athenians were so touched by the sight that they rewarded the donkey with free meals from the city rectorate, a symbolic honour reserved only for benefactors, official guests, and the victors of athletic games. And if the poor animal wanted to grab a bite from a stall at the market, no one was to stop it or harm it in any way.'

'What a touching tale! Alright, got it. The Parthenon was the bomb. Is this the reason that classical Athens is considered so important?'

'You wish. Not even close! The main reason was the unprecedented cultural creativity.'

'In what way?'

'Theatre, for one, really took off. The tragedies that are still renowned the world over were first performed under the Acropolis rock. Every year, the Athenians would gather for a large spring festival called the Greater or City Dionysia, as opposed to the Lesser Dionysia that took place in the various rural divisions of Attica. They would bring a packed lunch, park their behinds on the slopes under the Acropolis, and watch performance after performance for days on end, voting on which one they liked the best after it was all over. The winning playwright was awarded a tripod.'

'What a ridiculous gift! What would they do with it?'

'Why, what do people do today with an Oscar? I suppose it could be used as a doorstop to keep the kitchen door from slamming in the wind, although it's a stretch to say that is has any use beyond the symbolic. This is why the winning playwright often proudly planted his tripod on Tripodon Street.'

'Where was that street?'

'In downtown Athens, in the neighbourhood of Plaka, directly under the Acropolis – it's still there today, the same street with the same name.'

'You know, I read somewhere that many different peoples throughout the world held small religious theatrical performances earlier than the period of Classical antiquity.'

'That's correct.'

'Then why do the Greeks say that they created theatre?'

'Because those earlier religious performances were both rigidly prescribed and repetitive. It's in ancient Greece that for the first time in human history we see the use of a script and an audience that has no inkling of how the plot will unfold. They may be familiar with the myth they are watching, but the dialogue, the plot development, the twists and turns of the narrative are all new. What's more, the plays are simply brimming with emotion. In the Classical period, there are three greats – Aeschylus, Sophocles, and Euripides – who made theatre into what it is today.'

'Why were they so great?'

'Let's take them one by one.'

'Oh, please don't. It's sure to get boring.'

'But it won't, I promise you! They were all extremely interesting characters and it would be a pity to race through them. Aeschylus, the first of the three, started off as a humble vineyard labourer. One of his brothers, Cynaegirus, a live wire if ever there was one, is renowned for his heroic death in the Battle of Marathon, where he lunged at a Persian ship that was trying to get away.'

'You mean the one that the Persians kept hacking away at as they tried to escape?'

'The very same. The other brother led the attack against the Persian fleet in the naval Battle of Salamis.'

'Uh-huh. They seem like a very even-keeled bunch!'

'Well, someone else might call them heroic. Aeschylus, however, had nothing more to show for his participation in the war than regular and honourable service. At least, as far as we know. His inclinations, in any case, lay elsewhere. One night, Dionysus reputedly appeared to him in a dream and demanded that he write a play. Alarmed, the young man jolted up from his bed and immediately began writing his first work. It was his destiny to become an acclaimed tragic poet.'

'He was a poet? Didn't you just say that he wrote plays?'

'We call the authors of ancient plays tragic poets because they wrote tragedies that were not in prose but in verse or poetry. Aeschylus is therefore considered the father of tragedy.'

'But didn't you say that the other one, Thespis, was the father?'

'That's right. Aeschylus, however, changed the rules. He was the one to create an expectation for trilogies from each poet, and he also added a second actor to make the plot more interactive.'

'Whoa! You mean that until then only one person went out on stage?'

'Yes, and he would talk to the chorus. By adding a second actor, Aeschylus immediately made for a more interesting plot. He also stressed the importance of costumes, set design, every detail.'

'OK. Aeschylus was super important. What about the other two?'

'The second great tragic poet was Sophocles. He took the theatre even further. He added a third actor and increased character development.'

'A third? What a crowd! Haha!'

'He also won more tripods at the Dionysia than any other tragic poet.'

'And the third?'

'Third in line chronologically was Euripides. He was the one to introduce the *deus ex machina* to the theatre. He also steered clear of the great heroes of mythology, focusing instead on regular human beings, thus further amplifying the psychological depth of his characters. For the first time, the audience is treated to true psychological drama.'

'What is this *deus ex machina*? It sounds like an ice-cream maker!' He laughed.

'Yes, it was just as refreshing! Seriously, though, this is important. Ancient theatre is known for its confusions and complications, for plots that rapidly descend into big, tangled, disturbing messes. After all, they're tragedies, not sitcoms! They're really ripe, therefore, for someone with divine powers to step in and resolve the situation, to untangle the mess, or at least salvage what they can. This is why Euripides created a model that allows an actor to suddenly appear on stage as a god.'

'Like a superhero swooping in out of nowhere to save the day?'

'Either like a superhero, or a trapdoor that swings open – *whoosh* – to reveal a god who says, "Just a sec, my good people, I'm here to clean up the royal mess you've made of things."'

'Well, that's an easy out! There's nothing stopping you from writing the wildest, most improbable plots, because when things start to get hairy, all you have to do is bring in a god – there are at least a dozen, so you have plenty of choice! – and bing, bang, boom, everything has been resolved.'

'True. Which is why this particular theatrical device ought to be used only sparingly and with great discretion. In fact, it appears that even back in the day there were some demanding critics who were not very happy with it. It probably wasn't a general feeling, though; I'm sure that most of the audience heaved a sigh of relief whenever the god intervened.'

'Aha! So even back then we had that particular breed of know-it-all theatre enthusiast! Well, what I'm hearing is that classical Athens represents the pinnacle of ancient culture because it had the Parthenon and theatre. Anything else?'

'You're hard to please! Be careful what you wish for: no, theatre and the Parthenon were not the only things that Athens had to show for itself. In fact, around this time, it begins to draw the greatest minds from all over Greece. Scholars, historians, artists.'

'Every Tom, Dick, and Harry, eh? So what did they think was so great about Athens?'

'Most importantly, it now had a working democracy. And what does democracy thrive on? Dialogue and debate. This means that for the first time in history there's enormous cachet placed on the skillful, persuasive, and creative use of words. Sophistry and rhetoric are having their moment.'

'And was this only happening in Athens?'

'Not only in Athens, but Athens was certainly the hotbed. This obviously does not mean that there were no scholarly developments elsewhere. For example, Syracuse in Sicily is believed to be the birthplace of Corax, one of the founders of rhetoric, who happens to have a pretty funny name.'

'Corax? What does it mean?'

'*Corax* is the Greek word for crow. But the image of a cawing rhetorician is not the funniest thing about the name. There's a much more amusing anecdote about it that begins with a certain Tisias, who is seeking Corax out to offer a proposition: "Teacher, I don't have a penny to my name, but if you tutor me in the finer points of rhetoric, I will pay you back when I successfully argue my first case." Corax agrees, but once Tisias has learned all there is to learn, he refuses to exercise his rhetorical prowess in court and thus avoids having to make his payment. Corax is therefore forced to sue him, reasoning that regardless of the outcome of the case, he will get paid, for if Tisias loses the case, he is legally obliged to pay the fee he has promised, whereas if Tisias pleads his case successfully, he will, per their original agreement, still be bound to pay the fee. Tisias's counter-argument runs something like this: regardless of the outcome of the case, he will not owe anything, because if he wins the case, he will have to abide by the decision of the court that has acquitted him, whereas if he loses, he will have failed to successfully plead his case, and therefore, according to their original agreement, no payment is due. The judges can't make head or tail of it, so they simply declare: "the bad egg does not fall far from the bad crow".'

'Ha! Good one. What about philosophy? Is that also happening in Athens at this time?'

'The first philosophers, as we've already discussed, begin practising their craft in the colonies. They were natural philosophers, or philosophers interested in the workings of the natural and physical world. It was now time for philosophy to embrace all other aspects of life on earth beyond nature, including the human experience and the meaning of society, love, and death.

Which city in the Classical period do you think nurtured the development of philosophy more than any other?'

'Uh, let me guess . . . Clearly, it's Athens.'

'Ding, ding, ding! Correct! In Athens, then, we see the development of the new philosophy. There were three greats, whom you ought to remember.'

'Another trio?'

'Socrates, Plato, and Aristotle – in that order. The latter two were taught by their predecessor.'

'I'm still trying to remember Aeschylus, Sophocles, and Euripides. Now, you're asking me to remember the sequence for these three?'

'Here's a good mnemonic: the first letters of their names make the acronym SPA. Just remember that philosophy is the best and only SPA for the soul. In any case, Socrates is the greatest Athenian philosopher. Because of his influence on Plato, and Plato's on Aristotle, and their collective impact on all subsequent generations of philosophers, it's fair to say that Socrates was the father of philosophy.'

'Were Socrates's texts really all that important?'

'Socrates never wrote anything. He was known for his public, rather outspoken, declarations.'

'So how do we know what he said?'

'His pupils, chiefly Plato and Xenophon, wrote about him. Of course, it's quite possible that the first to transcribe Socrates's words was not one of his students, but a shoemaker, Simon.'

'A shoemaker? Like a cobbler?'

'Look, this is what appears to have happened: Socrates liked talking to young people; he was drawn to the freshness and openness of youth, to the urge to question and listen with a mind free of entrenched ideas. Yet young men who had not yet served in the army were not allowed into the ancient Agora –'

'Ah! I see where the saying "the army will make a man out of you" comes from!'

'These young men would frequent the shops along the Agora's periphery, and guess where Simon the shoemaker's shop was? Right there, outside the Agora. Despite his distaste for shoes, Socrates seems to have been a frequent visitor (even though he clearly never bought anything), and all the young men would gather around to talk to him. It probably did not take long before Simon was thinking to himself, "Hmm, this fellow certainly has the gift of the gab . . . How about I write it down and preserve it for future generations?" Naturally, none of the students who ended up writing about Socrates ever refer to Simon.'

'Why?'

'Possibly envy, perhaps disdain. We do see references to him, though, by later writers. There are reservations about his very existence, to say nothing of his writings. Archaeology, however, held yet another card up her sleeve, and during excavations of the ancient Agora, a structure was found on its periphery that contained tiny bone eyelets, perhaps used for holding string, and small nails used for shoe soles. There was also a small cup bearing an inscription saying that it belonged to a certain Simon. It looks like that building was the shoemaker's shop where Socrates liked to spend his time.'

'I still don't understand why everyone makes such a fuss about Socrates.'

'Socrates was much more than your run-of-the-mill philosopher. Firstly, he was a great warrior – I know this may seem irrelevant, but I mention it because I want you to get a sense of him as a complete person. One of the battles he fought in ended with an Athenian defeat, an utter rout, and Xenophon, the later historian and his student at the time, who had been fighting at his side, fell from his horse and was wounded. Socrates lifted him up onto his shoulders and got him out of the surrounding slaughter in one piece! He was also very quick on the draw. When some random stranger asked his advice about whether he ought to get married or not, Socrates replied that either way he would regret it. On another occasion, when his embarrassed wife was railing about receiving guests in their down-at-heel dump of a house, the unflappable philosopher, shot back: "If they are decent sorts, they won't give a damn about our house; if, on the other hand, they do give a damn, then giving a damn about what they think is an utter waste of time."'

'Ha! I like that. I'm going to use that line.'

'Socrates's brilliance, his relentless questioning of convention, ended up making him a thorn in the side of Athenian polite society, which then contrived to get him tried and sentenced to death. Hearing of the sentence, one of his friends protested, "Your death is unjust", and he replied, nonchalantly, "Would you like it any better if my death were just?"'

'I don't understand why they accused him of wrongdoing.'

'There were many reasons, and it's not something that can be covered in a few minutes, so just keep in mind that there were no fewer than three accusers at his trial: Meletus and Lycon, about whom we know very little, as well as Anytus, a tanner who blamed Socrates for trying to convince him to allow his son to study.'

'He didn't agree?'

'No, he wanted his son to become a tanner like himself, but Socrates wouldn't drop it and kept needling him. He made the wrong enemies and, at times, the wrong friends. He was charged, for example, for his former friendship with Critias. An adventurer who had been sent into exile, Critias returned to Athens in a position of authority in the short-lived dictatorship that was known as the coup of the Thirty Tyrants. He proceeded to have anyone he disliked executed without the benefit of a trial.'

'Socrates befriended him?'

'Not at that time. That's when they completely fell out and parted ways. In fact, Socrates did not hold back in his criticism of the tyrants. So Critias passed a law prohibiting anyone under the age of thirty to speak to Socrates.'

'What did Socrates do?'

'He laughed and said, "You mean that if the baker is younger than thirty years old, I can't buy a loaf of bread?"'

'If they were no longer friends, why did the court still hold it against him?'

'Give a dog a bad name and hang him. In any case, Socrates's thinking made a great impact on his students, the most famous of whom was Plato.'

'OK. Tell me about him.'

'Plato was a real powerhouse of a student, which is why they called him Plato, from the Greek word *platís* for wide, because he was rather stout. Legend has it that some bees gently rested on the sleeping infant Plato's lips as he lay in his crib, an omen of the sweetness that those lips would impart on the world.'

'Ha! They all had legends about their childhood, didn't they? You don't really hear, "Oh, that one – all he did was fill his nappy!"'

'Well, I'm not saying that he didn't regularly fill his nappy. He must have done that too. After the death of his teacher

Socrates, the now adult Plato became his most famous student, the one who ended up making Socrates a household name and the protagonist of most of his texts. You see, Plato's texts weren't dry philosophical treatises but dialogues, novels of sorts. He also founded the world's first university, the Academy or Akademia, in the fields outside Athens's city walls, among beautiful groves of olive trees, near the sanctuary for the hero Academus.'

'Could you explain in simple language what Plato's philosophy was about?'

'His philosophy was not simple, nor is it easily summarised without doing it a disservice. It was a work in progress that he kept evolving and modifying during his entire lifetime.'

'Well, then, just give me a highlight or two. What should I know about Plato?'

'OK, if you truly just want the highlights, I recommend his Allegory of the Cave, in which he explains the origins of human ignorance, why it is so difficult to combat, and the human predilection for conservatism and fear of the new.'

'Go on.'

'Suppose we all lived chained to the wall of a cave deep in the ground, facing a blank wall. Up above, suspended high in the cave, burns a light, in front of which swing various objects, thus casting their shadows on the wall. Those shadows are the only world we know. Now say that someone, wishing to open your eyes to the truth, breaks your chains and leads you up to the surface. Initially, after having spent an entire lifetime sitting in that dark, damp cave, your rigid and atrophied muscles make the climb painful, agonising. Kicking and screaming, after terrible torment, you make it to the exit; the light blinds you; you're thoroughly dazed. Not only are you in pain, now you're also unable to see. But you're resilient, you survive. What do you do? All the things you knew only as vague shadows now stand before you in their full, vivid reality: shock and horror. You think you've lost your mind. Even though the full perception of truth is hard, you endure, you manage not to succumb to madness. Then, it occurs to you, "Hey, I must rouse the others who are still slaves to a lie!" You go down to the cave to reveal the truth. Now accustomed to the light, you can no longer see in all that darkness. You stumble and limp along, a laughable sight to those whose eyes are inured to the paltry light. They listen to you as you try to sow doubt in everything they ever held to be true, but your words make no sense. Who are you to question their truth, their faith in the shadows they've known all their lives? You, who are stumbling and falling and seem to have lost control of your senses? It stands to reason that they will either turn a deaf ear or despise you. This, in a nutshell, is the Allegory of the Cave. Applied to today in real and simple terms, this allegory speaks to why it's still difficult to defeat stereotypes and ideologies like racism and sexism that are deeply rooted and transmitted from generation to generation. If you want more of Plato, you will have to invest the time and read him carefully. Throughout this period, philosophy continues to evolve and become more complex as a discipline.'

'You mean because of Socrates's and Plato's work?'

'As well as Aristotle's, the third person in the trio.'

'Was he cut from the same cloth as the other two?'

'Not exactly. Aristotle hailed from Stagira, a colony of Andros in today's central Macedonia. He was orphaned at a very young age, but because he came from wealth, he was able to travel to Athens and study at Plato's Academy. While Aristotle was not chosen as Plato's heir to the Academy when the latter died, he did receive an extraordinary job offer from King Philip II of Macedon, who invited him to found a "private school" for the heir to the Macedonian throne, Alexander.'

'He accepted?'

'He accepted, and in exchange Philip rebuilt Aristotle's hometown, which had been razed to the ground by the Macedonians.'

'Ouch! And he actually founded a school with only one student?'

'Alexander was the excuse for the school, but he was not the only student. Classes were attended by the wealthy sons of the Macedonian aristocracy. This was the generation that, party to Alexander the Great's lengthy military campaigns, was soon to change the course of world history. When they graduated, Aristotle closed down this school and founded a new one further to the south, open to a broader clientele – the Lyceum in Athens. Aristotle was a polymath who was voraciously curious about the world, studying philosophy, zoology, botany, political science, poetry, music, theatre. Indeed, it's fair to say that he was the first Renaissance man. Sadly, most of his writings have been lost. The bulk of what remains to us today essentially consists of his class notes or plans for the Lyceum.'

'Oof, this has turned into a philosophy lesson! Weren't you talking to me about archaeology?'

'Alright, my friend, coming right up! Where were we? Ah, yes, the Classical period brought important changes to art, and chiefly to sculpture. The now corny, almost ironic Archaic smile is a thing of the past, and statues become rather p-p-p-poker-faced (thank you, Lady Gaga!). This is why the dominant sculptural idiom of the time is known as the Severe style. Naturally, that was not the only thing that changed.'

'What else?'

'I don't remember if I've already mentioned this but, in general, ancient Greek art was not given to fixity, conservatism. It appears that Greek artists bored easily and were always eager for new challenges. As a result, art kept changing, evolving at regular intervals, approximately every quarter-century, more or less.'

'Why every quarter-century? Was there a reason?'

'There's a very simple reason. With each new generation of artists, we see the preservation of certain aspects of the styles they had been taught, as well as attempts to outdo their teachers and create something better. Statues in this period are freed from the now clichéd moulds and attitudes of the Archaic period, and we see the introduction of *contrapposto* in sculpture.'

'OK, see what you just did? You threw out that term as if it were the most self-evident thing in the world. Haven't you realised that even when you use English jargon, I have a hard time of it. How do you expect me to make any sense of Latin?'

'*Contra* – or counter – and *posto* – or pose – gives us the word "counterpoise". Archaic statues, as you've probably noticed, are remarkable for how unnaturally rigid and straight they stand. In the Classical period, statues no longer look as if they've got a stick up their you-know-what. Sculptors begin to place most of the figure's weight on one leg, relax the other one, and twist the shoulders off axis, so that the figure's sides and the line of the shoulders in relation to the hips are asymmetrical – in counterpoise. Think of how we stand in line at the bank and what the body looks like when it's relaxed or in motion. Classical artists are now free to do what they want with the human body. Let's take the ancient sculptor Ageladas as an example. And I will have you know that his name means cow in Greek, but please spare me the witticisms!'

'Oh, come on! You're having me on. Was that really his name?'

'It was indeed, my friend! An unfortunate name, it's true, but he is reputed to have been an exceptional sculptor; and reputation, sadly, is all we have to go on, because none of his work survives. Even though he was a sculptor of the Archaic period, all his students were active in the Classical. Phidias, of Parthenon-sculpture fame, was the most renowned. Then we have Myron, creator of the famous *Discobolus*, an extraordinary exemplar of the body in its full range of motion. Twisting and bending like an elastic band, the athlete is a split-second away from throwing the discus and amazing his fans. There's also Polykleitos, who, besides his one acclaimed statue, *Doryphoros*—'

'*Doryphoros*? What a strange word! What on earth does it mean?'

'It's the word for satellite in modern Greek, but since ancient times it has also meant spear-bearer. Don't get them confused, though! The statue was not made to orbit the earth. It was called *Doryphoros* because the figure was holding a spear, or a *dory* in Greek. He who comes bearing (*phore*) a spear (*dory*) gives us *doryphoros*, or spear-bearer. Even though, once again, the original statue has been lost, it has been copied hundreds of times since its creation and is considered the model for the ideal proportions of the male human figure – Polykleitos even wrote a book about it! Polykleitos the Younger, architect of the famous theatre at Epidaurus, may have been his son. And since we're on the subject of architecture, a time-honoured and esteemed profession since antiquity, I ought to mention that many architects wrote about their own work. For example, Theodorus, who built the Tholos, an odd, circular temple at Delphi, wrote such a book.'

'Do we still have it?'

'No such luck. That too was lost.'

'So we don't know what that circular building was all about?'

'No, it remains a mystery. A similar circular building also exists at Epidaurus. It was built by Polykleitos the Younger, who also built the theatre. For that matter, we don't know that much about how the theatre was used.'

'Were they still adding those classical pillars to everything?'

'They're not called classical pillars!'

'OK, whatever – the Doric and Ionic styles that you were talking about earlier.'

'Mainly, yes, but during the Classical period we see the introduction of the third major order of antiquity, the Corinthian. Legend has it that the sculptor Callimachus was wandering around outside Corinth when he spotted the tomb of a young girl—'

'Hang on – why would he take a walk in a cemetery?'

'Look, in antiquity it was almost inevitable, because cemeteries were placed outside the city walls to prevent the spread of disease. Infectious disease, after all, was a major cause of death, and, more broadly, death was associated with contamination and bad luck. Therefore, the two worlds, those of the living and the dead, had to be kept strictly apart. At the same time, because the dead – as one's ancestors and relatives – were due proper honour and commemoration, they were buried next to the roads leading into the city. This is why on many ancient tombstones we see epigraphs addressing the traveller or passer-by. Besides, a sure way to strike below the belt during the countless conflicts among Greeks in antiquity was either to destroy a cemetery – the Aetolians did it to the Macedonians – or to transplant the city's dead somewhere else, thus depriving their heirs of their forebears and leaving them rootless – the Athenians did this to the Delians. On the whole, though, this type of thing was quite rare because it was considered a terrible sacrilege.'

'Yeah, that just made my skin crawl. Let's get back to Callimachus's walk outside Corinth.'

'Alright, so, as Callimachus is strolling around, he spots a young girl's grave with a cone-shaped basket on it. The basket contains all the toys and personal effects that the child, in her brief life, had not had the time to fully enjoy. Abandoned there for years on the neglected burial, the wicker basket has succumbed to the forces of nature and is entwined with the leaves of an acanthus plant. This image is said to have inspired Callimachus to create the most elaborate of all capitals in antiquity, the Corinthian capital.'

'Okey dokey. So, if I've understood you correctly, in a nutshell, after the war, ancient Greece is caught in a frenzy of development.'

'That's right. In the first fifty years after the Persian Wars – also known as the Pentecontaetia – we see a truly vertiginous growth in the arts, knowledge, and trade. And what happens when so many new pathways are forged in culture, the arts, and the branches of human knowledge?'

'What?'

'Well, naturally . . . civil war.'

'Are you being ironic?'

'Obviously! Athens's rapid ascent alarmed Sparta and her allies, and the resulting Peloponnesian Wars, which lasted for twenty-seven years, from 431 to 404 BCE, were so pervasive that the rest of Greece was obliged to choose a side. Almost three decades of uninterrupted war, during which one side would weary and call for peace, only to have the other side opportunistically strike all the harder, thus keeping the merry-go-round spinning on and on endlessly.'

'Which side won?'

'Sparta.'

'I'm sorry, but . . . how? I mean, Athens was a force to be reckoned with, with its powerful fleet and alliances, and the peerless Pericles at the helm.'

'Pericles succumbed to the plague that struck Athens in the early years of the war. The city was literally brought to its knees. Despite the fact that it managed to catch its breath and even occasionally looked like it might win the war, Athens ultimately buckled and its alliances dissolved. Democracy fell and was replaced by the tyrannical government of the Thirty Tyrants, who proceeded to order mass executions of any Athenians still loyal to democratic ideals and, more generally, anyone with whom they didn't see eye-to-eye.'

'Ugh! Did this government last long?'

'Fortunately, no. The Athenians were constitutionally unable to live under a dictatorship for too long. In a matter of months, the people revolted, the Thirty were sent packing, and democracy was restored. Gradually, tentatively, Athens tried to rally and heal the wounds of war and political turmoil, but it took years. A real gem from this period is the famed tombstone depicting a horseman killing his foe.'

'That reminds me of Saint George or other Christian saints doing battle on their horses.'

'That's right. This motif of the horseman is an enduring one that we also see in the art of the Christian period, when saints are depicted on horseback, killing dragons and other adversaries.'

'Is this why the tombstone is of interest?'

'Among other reasons. It belonged to a young cavalryman, Dexileos, who died in a battle in Corinth just after turning twenty. This is the only surviving monument from ancient Athens that records the dates of birth and death.'

'It wasn't customary?'

'No.'

'So why did they do it for Dexileos?'

'Because he died a few years after the regime of the Thirty Tyrants. Keep in mind that the tyrants obviously were not fishermen, farmers, or manual labourers; they were aristocrats, knights. To put it another way, they had the resources necessary to keep horses for war. The young cavalryman's family therefore clearly wanted to make it known that the boy was only eleven years old when the Tyrants assumed power, that he was in no way involved or to blame for the aristocrats' debacle.'

'What happened when the civil war ended?'

'The end of the Peloponnesian Wars also brings an end to the glorious fifth century – Pericles's "Golden Age", as you pointed out – which leaves us, as the curtains close, with the sight of Athens licking its wounds and the Greek world thoroughly reeling from relentless conflict. Sparta, in the meantime, is under the illusion that it has regained pride of place and is holding the reins to all other Greek cities. In actual fact, arrogance has gone to her head, for it is now the turn of another city to take centre stage. A few years later, entirely by chance, Thebes becomes the birthplace of not one but two brilliant military minds, Epaminondas and Pelopidas. As a result, the formerly provincial Thebes expands its military and becomes the most powerful city in Greece, albeit for a few years only.'

'The story of an outsider triumph, eh?'

'Among other things – but it is true that Thebes achieved the impossible when it vanquished Sparta. It was the first time that an external army was able to imperil Sparta, the only Greek city without walls.'

'Sparta had no fortification walls?'

'It didn't need them when it had Spartan warriors! Even though the Theban army did not succeed in fully entering the city, Sparta lost control over its own backyard in the Peloponnese. Entire regions like Messenia and Arcadia, enslaved by Sparta for centuries, gained their independence and established new capital cities, Messene and Megalopolis respectively. But when Thebes lost its invincible duo, Epaminondas and Pelopidas, it also lost its leadership of Greek affairs.'

'Which city took over?'

'In that period, Athens tried to retake the helm. It worked to rebuild its former alliances with almost the entire Aegean, this time with a lighter and less oppressive hand, for it was cognisant of the fact that if its allies weren't happy, they would abandon ship. Of course, it never fully regained its former power.'

'Am I right in assuming that all that conflict brought an end to their cultural achievements?'

'No, the arts did not come to a standstill – they continued to evolve, as did philosophy and the branches of knowledge. You may find it surprising, but keep in mind that even though the Peloponnesian Wars were the period's equivalent to a world war, people at that time had never really experienced complete peace. Yes, it was a large-scale conflict between two opposing blocks, but both before and after it, the Greek world was rife with localised and isolated skirmishes, battles, and wars. Arts, culture, scholarship, all still bloomed against this background.'

'This is all great, mate, but I need to say something: the problem with all you archaeologists, historians, and scholarly types in general is that you browbeat us with a whole lot of big words and endless analyses, but you say nothing about the real people involved in it all. Where are they?'

'They're everywhere, in everything I've just talked about.'

'I don't see it! All this time, all you've done is talk generally about history and culture! Again, I ask, where are the people?'

'You need to learn to pay better attention to the details. When you do, you will see the people, vivid and vibrant, living lives of joy, success, horror, pain, bereavement, even in the most unassuming of things. As an example, let's go back to Athens in this period and look at a series of legal speeches authored by Pseudo-Demosthenes.'

'What do you mean by legal speeches? And which period, exactly, are we talking about? After the Peloponnesian War? Also, by the way, who is this Pseudo-Demosthenes?'

'Yes, we are now looking at the period after the war, and "legal speech" refers to the indictments lodged by Athenian citizens in the courts of law. Finally, Demosthenes was a famous rhetorician and politician. It turns out, though, that some of the surviving speeches attributed to him weren't actually his. Hence, they're pseudo-Demosthenic works.'

'Why did they say they were his in the first place?'

'For the prestige, my friend! In any case, one of these speeches reveals a truly incredible, well-nigh unimaginable story involving a slave, a prostitute, and a thoroughly neurotic politician.'

'Well, I can already guess that they weren't friends . . . so was the slave the property of the politician?'

'No, he was the politician's father! Pasion – that was his name – who was foreign-born, probably from Syria or thereabouts, belonged to the two Athenian owners of a small bank in Piraeus. He was so good at his job and so effective at growing the bank's business that his masters granted him not only his freedom but, when they stepped down, the entire bank. Pasion's wife, Archippe, was also a shrewd and capable character, and together they built the most powerful bank in Athens, while also starting a successful shield-production business. Indeed, at one point, when the city found itself in need, they donated thousands of shields along with – wait for it – an entire warship! To cut a long story short, for his sizeable contributions, Pasion was awarded the honorary title of Athenian citizen, and both his sons were made citizens as well.'

'What about his wife?'

'It looks like his wife never became a citizen. Women did not have political rights in ancient Athens. Interestingly, when Pasion died at around sixty years of age, he did not leave the business to his then-twenty-four-year-old elder son, Apollodorus, but instead to his freed slave, Phormion. The latter ended up marrying the widowed Archippe and assuming guardianship of the other son, who was still underage. Together, then, Phormion and Archippe continued running the business.'

'So Apollodorus was completely cut out?'

'Yes. Despite the fact that he still had plenty of wealth at his disposal and had married into the nobility, the arrangement continued to rankle. He took Phormion to court and lost. Now, hold on to that information, because at this point, we need to take a small detour and go to Corinth in the same period, to the dwelling place of Neaira, a prostitute.'

'Why are you jumping from one to the other?'

'Wait and see. You're the one who asked, "Where are the people?" So, as I was saying, Neaira, probably orphaned early in life, fell into the clutches of a Corinthian madam who was known for presenting her brothel's young courtesans as her daughters – basically, a pretext to charge top dollar. Over time, Madam Nikarete toured the beautiful Neaira far and wide outside Corinth, including to cities like Athens, which was then awash with wealth. This is where the girl met Phrynion, a young man who took quite a liking to her. On their return to Corinth, however, Nikarete struck a deal with two good friends who wanted to buy the girl and share her. Indeed, because one of them was still living with his mother, they had her live in the other's house. This arrangement lasted until the two young men decided to settle down, at which point they offered the hapless Neaira the opportunity to buy her own freedom.'

'And she paid? Did she have that kind of money?'

'As you correctly imagine, no, she did not have the money, so she requested the help of the Athenian Phrynion, who was still quite keen on her. Phrynion did pay up, but instead of freeing her, as she had thought, he took her to Athens and started selling her there. The despairing girl managed to run off to Megara, a neighbouring city, where she met a certain Stephanus, who seems to have been the only one of her "suitors" to truly fall in love with her. Together, they return to Athens, and when Neaira's ex, Phrynion, hears about it, he attempts to take her back by force. Stephanus, true to his lover's vows, staves him off, so they take the matter to court and something truly unprece-dented happens: the judges rule that Neaira does not belong to anyone, that she is her own mistress. For ancient Athens, this was truly revolutionary.'

'So all's well that ends well?'

'Not on your life! Stephanus, it turns out, is all pretty talk and no action, a penniless loafer, and Neaira is forced to go back to prostitution to support them and the children.'

'His or hers?'

'We don't know whose exactly. Then, things take another turn when Stephanus serves as a witness in a suit brought by Apollodorus, the son of the freed slave turned wealthy banker, against Phormion, the inheritor of the business. Remember? Well, this is where the two stories converge. Because Steph-anus serves as a witness for Phormion, who ends up winning the case, he is caught in Apollodorus's crosshairs. It also can't have helped that they were in opposing political parties . . . In any case, Apollodorus makes it his mission to wreak vengeance on the wretched Stephanus.'

'Apollodorus sounds like a really neurotic and litigious type, doesn't he?'

'Impossible to say for certain, but the fact that his father refused to leave him the business, and his mother and brother were not on his side, does give one pause, doesn't it?'

'Did Apollodorus get his revenge?'

'He tried to indirectly, by maligning Neaira. There was a renowned trial in which Apollodorus indicted the courtesan by exposing her entire life and times to the court, providing a full account of all the "tours" she'd taken and the filth of her life as a prostitute. Neaira, now close to fifty, was likely present during the proceedings, but as a woman she was not allowed to speak.

All she could do was sit there and listen to the accusations. If Apollodorus won, she was in danger of losing everything and being sold into slavery.'

'Was she acquitted or not?'

'We don't know. If found guilty, it's very likely that she lost everything and ended up a slave somewhere, so it's not surprising that we lose track of her.'

'What do you mean you don't know? I can't take the suspense. How can you leave me hanging at the most critical part?'

'That's what it's like to work on antiquity, my friend. We're still missing so many pieces of the puzzle. This is why our work feeds the imagination and the thinking process.'

'Well, that was quite a gripping story of the slave, the courtesan, and the big sore loser of a son!'

'I do think it's quite likely that Apollodorus lost the case. After all, he had lost others, and doesn't seem to have been cut out for success. We wouldn't be too off-target in trusting that Neaira was acquitted. In any case, I hope you see now how the stories of regular people's lives are always there, running parallel to history's great events.'

'Alright, let's get back to the bigger picture: Athens was tired, Sparta was tired, and Thebes was a one-hit wonder. Who grabbed the reins to the Greek world?'

'In the middle of the fourth century BCE it was time for the ascent of a new power: Macedonia.'

'Was Macedonia a city-state like the others?'

'Unlike the Greeks of the south, northern Greeks formed kingdoms instead of city-states. Most of northern Greece was occupied by the kingdoms of Epirus, Thessaly, and Macedonia. Macedonia was a small kingdom that was often beleaguered from all sides. During the Peloponnesian War, Athens and

Sparta ransacked it for the timber and other raw materials that were essential to the navy and the general war effort. It also suffered incursions from Thrace, Illyria, and all its Balkan neighbours, as well as from the Thebans who, as mentioned earlier, held the reigns to the Greek world for a short while.'

'But until the Classical period, Macedonia was small potatoes?'

'No, not at all! Intermittently, capable monarchs fortified the kingdom, the most important of whom was Archelaus, under whose watch the capital was transferred from Aigai to Pella. After Archelaus, however, the kingdom went through a long and difficult period. Generally, its neighbours rode roughshod all over it for quite some time. Until Philip II assumed the throne, that is, because he, too, was a force to be reckoned with. He inherited a kingdom that was literally in ruins, and in a matter of a few years this fireball of a man had not only found a way to revive his half-dead realm, but to strengthen it to such an extent that it dominated all others. As had always been the case, when a certain power won supremacy over Greek land, the rest would form a coalition against it. In 338 BCE, the last coalition against Philip II went to battle with him in Chaeronea in Boeotia. Thanks to the manoeuvres of Philip's young son and prince of Macedon, Alexander, who led the Macedonian cavalry in the battle, the Macedonian forces won a resounding victory. Soon after that, Alexander ascended to the throne of Macedonia and what followed was beyond anyone's wildest dreams. With the precipitous rise of Alexander's star, Greece finally breached its boundaries, and the Classical period came to an end. The phenomenon known as Alexander the Great left behind a new world that was to become known as Hellenistic.'

'OK, let's see what I remember of that torrent of information you just battered me with. The Classical period began with the Greek victory in the Persian Wars and ended with Macedonian dominion over the Greek mainland.'

'That's right! And what of note happened during this period?'

'An incredible growth in the culture and arts, and, of course, that endless Peloponnesian War.'

'Exactly! Now listen to this, and you'll see how closely cultural and military histories are intertwined. Remember how we talked about the three great tragic poets – Aeschylus, Sophocles, and Euripides? By a strange twist of fate, the lives of these great artists span the entire Classical period and connect all the dots we just discussed. First off, they represent the highest art of the period: theatre, rhetoric, philosophy, inquiry. Furthermore, while Aeschylus is associated with the Persians and the beginning of the Classical period, Sophocles is associated with the Peloponnesian Wars in the middle of the period, and Euripides with the period's end and the new emergent power, the kingdom of Macedonia.'

'What do you mean, they're "associated"?'

'Aeschylus died in an accident in distant southern Italy, in the ancient colony of Gela, when, according to legend, an eagle, mistaking his bald head for a rock, dropped a turtle on it. The only thing he wanted inscribed on his tomb was that he too, just like his brothers, had fought in the Battle of Marathon to defend hearth and home from the Persian invasion that heralded the birth of classical Greece, and which he had written about in one of his tragedies, *The Persians*. It's the oldest surviving theatrical play in the world, and it tells a tale that the poet himself had actually experienced firsthand. This tragedy was Aeschylus's first win, and his sponsor was the young Pericles, later to become politician and ruler of Athens during the period of her greatest glory. Now, let's look at Sophocles. Legend has it that he died during the time of the Peloponnesian War, either while eating grapes or in an attempt to recite a long verse of the tragedy *Antigone* without pausing for breath. When he died, Athens was under siege by the Spartans. Because the cemeteries were outside the city walls and the Athenians were confined within them for the duration of the war, the Spartans agreed to cease hostilities and permit the burial of the renowned poet.'

'You mean there is at least one moment in time in the history of civilisation when art managed to stop a war, even if only for a day?'

'Exactly. Finally Euripides – who was born, again according to legend, on the very day of the naval Battle of Salamis, and was known for writing the most humanistic of ancient dramas – left Athens because he could no longer stomach his fellow citizens; to be frank, he looks to have been a bit of a misanthrope! He spent the last years of his life in the rustic court of King Archelaus of Macedon, a man of culture who hosted all the artistic crème de la crème of the period. Euripides wrote the tragedy *Archelaus* in his honour, and there, in the fertile, creative soil of Macedonia, he also wrote his renowned *Bacchae*. He came to a terrible end, torn apart by dogs while taking a walk in the countryside, and so remained there forever, part of the Macedonian soil that had nurtured him, in the Macedonia which, under the firm hand of Alexander the Great, was to disseminate Greek culture beyond the boundaries of Greece and throughout the world, thus bringing an end to antiquity's Classical period and inaugurating the Hellenistic period.'

'Can I stop you with another question? Would finding Alexander the Great's tomb truly be the ultimate triumph for an archaeologist?'

'I should have expected that question. OK, listen – I'll tell you what an archaeologist's top priority is in terms of finds.'

FAQ

What is an Excavation's Most Important Find?

'BEFORE YOU JUMP to conclusions, I want to make one thing clear: it's not a particular object. An excavation's key discovery, the "find" that provides us with critical information that can help us with the interpretation of everything else, is its stratigraphy.'

'What is that?'

'As we've already talked about, over the centuries, archaeological sites are covered by strata of earth. These strata provide important information that helps us understand the nature and date of the site's occupation. How long was it occupied? For how many centuries? In which periods? Was it inhabited in prehistory, abandoned for a while, and then repopulated in the Classical period? Or did the repopulation take place during the Roman period? When we carefully examine a site's strata, they help us answer a host of questions with direct evidence: what does each stratum contain? In which stratum was a particularly rare find located? When was this wall built? When was it levelled? What is the date of this trench? What did it contain? When was it covered over? Besides, once you have established a secure context, a well-defined stratigraphic unit, in other words, you are able to classify and locate your finds. You do not need to worry about the date of a vase or a statue. The strata attest to it.'

'Ah, so it's that simple!'

'Stratigraphy is not a simple thing. But its logic is, very much so. Imagine a stack of three books on a table. The book at the bottom of the stack is the one that was first placed on the table and is therefore the "oldest". The book at the top of the stack is the "youngest". The book in the middle is more recent than the book on the bottom, but older than the book on top. This principle applies to the layers of the earth. Of course, in practice, it is never this simple because we are not talking about only three layers but rather tens or hundreds that are not evenly distributed over the archaeological site. Nor are they necessarily easy to distinguish. Not to mention the fact that over the centuries, someone is sure to have dug either a well or a rubbish dump, for example, and when such holes are dug, older earth is brought to the surface. When they are filled, of course, "younger" materials end up deeper than they should be.'

'So how do you tell the strata apart?'

'By a very careful analysis. An experienced archaeologist is able to distinguish between the different layers and any disturbances they may have experienced throughout the entire archaeological site: a well in one corner, for example, or the hollows left by the beams used to build a cabin or support a canopy – that sort of thing.'

'But don't you risk overlooking something, either by confusing the strata or completely missing one of them?'

'Yes, that's a very real risk. This is why excavation, like surgery, has to be a painstakingly careful process. The priority is not to bulldoze through and get to whatever is still there underground! This is why illicit archaeological excavations destroy more than we can imagine, and we lose critical information that could potentially tell us a lot about antiquity. To understand the damage they cause, picture a large layer cake that someone has run a fork through and mashed. Conversely, when the strata are secure and undisturbed – in other words, no one has dug there relatively recently – then the finds in each stratum can help us determine how old they are.'

'Give me an example.'

'Here's a simplified one. You are excavating a site that has five layers. In the first layer, right up on top, you find ceramics from the Byzantine period; in the second, you find a Roman epigraph; in the third, Hellenistic ceramics; the fourth contains black-figure vases from the Classical period; and the fifth, Mycenaean vases. In other words, you have a site that spans from the Mycenaean to the Byzantine eras. Now, if you find something, whether it's a key or a skull, depending on the layer where it was found, you will know what period it hails from.'

'I thought that archaeologists dig to find things.'

'We do dig for things, but that's far from our only goal. We do not necessarily excavate in search of the impressive find or the beautiful sculpture. This is not to say, of course, that it's not a thrill and great surprise when we do happen on something like that, but we are not hunters of ancient works of art. We look for much more; most of all, ways to answer our questions.'

'In other words, even when you don't find any objects, there's some meaning in it.'

'Yes. For example, if you're digging in the middle of a big ancient city and you find nothing, that's critical information. I mean, why is there nothing – just a large pit of sand – in a city centre? What could be the reason for such an open public space? Was it the site for some form of construction that did not survive the test of time? Makeshift wooden benches, perhaps, that were assembled and disassembled as needed? Is this where Mrs. Homemaker went to buy her fruit and veg at the outdoor market? Or where the community would gather for a good dance, like an outdoor rave? The lack of finds does not mean a lack of questions, answers, inferences. So in a nutshell, yes, finding Alexander the Great's tomb would be terribly interesting, but in no way is it the only thing that concerns us as a discipline.'

'Are you going to finally tell me about Alexander the Great, then?'

10

Wrecking Ball
(Alexander the Great)

'ALEXANDER III, Alexander the Great, the Conqueror of the World, the Philosopher King, my man Alex. Needless to say, the laurels of greatness are conferred on particular historical figures for reasons that are often both partisan and debatable. That's not the case with Alex. In my humble opinion, Alex deserves every bit of it.'

'Why are you calling him Alex? Isn't it a little . . . derogatory?'

'Why is using a diminutive derogatory? Where do these strange perceptions of impropriety come from? As is probably clear, I am a huge fan of Alex's, and I'm sure he couldn't have cared less about whether I idolise or insult him. After all, it's indisputable that he changed the course of world history like very few before or after him. Besides, I don't believe that putting history on a pedestal is at all useful. History does not call for the unnecessary distractions of awe and reverence. I am a proponent of becoming intimately acquainted with the past and approaching it with an easy familiarity.'

'Yes, OK, I've heard you say things like that before. Yet you yourself have put Alex, as you call him, on a pedestal. Why are you such of fan of his? When all is said and done, wasn't he just a glorified butcher?'

'I haven't put him on a pedestal, and I don't see his life through rose-tinted glasses; I see it as it really was, and I still find it impressive. Furthermore, why single out Alex as a "butcher"? As opposed to any other leader of either ancient or, for that matter, more recent history? Either we agree that they're all butchers or, since all of history is basically a protracted blood-bath, we agree to judge fairly and consistently without singling out just one of the countless butchers out there.'

'But given all his military campaigns, didn't Alexander the Great kill more people than all of them put together?'

'Interesting point, and since you bring it up, I can tell you that Alex inflicted much less harm than many other military leaders. He fought far fewer wars, treated those he vanquished with greater mercy, and tried to steer clear of armed conflict as much as possible. He was certainly no saint, but neither was he a demon. He was a brilliant, extraordinarily gifted young man who, after a certain point, started to buy into his own legend and let it go to his head. Hard not to do when you've conquered the entire world and you're barely an adult!'

'What I know is that he waged violent and expansionist wars.'

'He waged war against the Persian Empire. He did what many had dreamed of doing; something that had been brewing for centuries. The Greek world and the Persian Empire had been embroiled in a strange tug-of-war from the time of the Persian Wars. Despite its loss then, Persia had never stopped meddling in Greek affairs and trying to indirectly manipulate the Greek world. Who do you think gave Sparta the gold required to build her fleet and vanquish Athens in the Peloponnesian War? None other than Persia, my friend! Overall, the point is that one hundred and fifty years after the Persian Wars, the Greeks and the Persians were still locked in a "cold war". Alex's big moment came when the Greeks finally girded their loins and decided to take the fight to the Persians' home turf.

'But let's take Alex's story from the beginning, with his unexpected ascent to the Macedonian throne. True, he was the lawful heir, but at the time he was barely out of his adolescence and not on the best of terms with his father, Philip II, who had recently remarried and looked to have many hale and hearty years as king ahead of him. Indeed, he was planning an attack on Greece's longstanding foe, the Persian Empire, and had gathered the Greeks in Corinth to create the League of Corinth, whose goal was to end enmities among the Greek states in order to unify them against Persia. In essence, Philip was the first to succeed in uniting the Greek states under one banner.'

'All of them?'

'Not all. A small village in central Laconia called Sparta refused to comply.'

'You mean just like Asterix's village refused to surrender to the Roman Empire in *Asterix and Obelix vs. Caesar*?'

'Yes, except that the entire set of characters and their daily lives were a lot less comic. Sparta certainly was no laughing matter, especially when provoked: the city retained all its old arrogance. After Philip had vanquished everyone and brought them over to his side, Sparta remained a lone holdout, so he sent them a message: "If I conquer Sparta, I will show no mercy." The Spartan response was a laconic "If".'

'And the Spartans got away with this arrogance?'

'Even though they lacked their former strength, no one was eager to lock horns with them given their centuries-long reputation as the regional toughs. In any case, Philip chose to respect Sparta, and he turned a blind eye while he gathered all the other Greeks in Corinth and they formed their confederacy. Shortly thereafter, he organised a massive shindig for his daughter's wedding in his kingdom's former capital, Aigai, with a guestlist brimming with VIPs from all over the Greek world. Dressed all in white, Philip presided over an unprecedented spectacle at the Aigai theatre: statues of the twelve gods were paraded before an audience hailing from every corner of Greek land. As the last statue of the gods filed past, a thirteenth appeared before the crowd's startled eyes: it was a statue of Philip.'

'Ha! So he was playing god now?'

'Yes, it was terrible hubris and he paid for it almost immediately. An assassin dashed out of the crowd, stabbed him, and left him for dead.'

'On account of the hubris, or some other reason?'

'The reason for the murder remains unclear, nor do we know who ordered the killing. In any case, the great king was dead, and twenty-year old Alex suddenly found himself heir to the most powerful state in Greece at the time.

'Everyone was probably thinking "Oh, my, what's that nipper doing on the throne! Macedonia's days are numbered." The League of Corinth began to fall apart. The first to rebel and defect was Thebes, after hearing and believing a false rumour that the young Macedonian had been killed in a battle with the Thracians. Athens, in the meantime, strongly seconded the Thebans' intention to abandon the confederacy and both encouraged and supported them. Alex, however, was not one to let this sort of thing get him down; he had other plans up his sleeve, and it wouldn't take long before everyone was in for a big surprise. In record time, he and his troops were outside the Theban walls. "Wake up, Thebes, you've bitten off more than you can chew." Undeterred, Thebes stood her ground, and Alex had no other choice but to take the city. History tells us that he then razed it to the ground in retaliation, even though, in actuality, he had left the decision to the Boeotian Federation; in other words, the remaining Boeotian city-states bordering Thebes. Having endured much from the more powerful Thebes, they were the ones to mandate its destruction. Alex's lone interventions were to ask that the poet Pindar's house be spared and to forgive Athens for its role in the Theban revolt.'

'Why did he forgive Athens?'

'Because Alexander had studied with Aristotle and therefore knew that Athens had nurtured and inspired the ancient world's greatest thinkers. In other words, it was Athens's prestige that saved her. Shortly after that, Alex makes his way to Asia in pursuit of both his father's ambition and the dream that so many in Greece had harboured ever since the Persian Wars had come to a close one hundred and fifty years earlier: to vanquish the Persian Empire.'

'Why hadn't their beef ended with the Persian Wars?'

'Hard to tell, but it hadn't. It's true that the Persian Wars had ended with a Greek victory, but, as I've already mentioned, Persia had been trying to undermine and indirectly meddle in Greek affairs ever since. The first battle takes place at the River Granicus, and even though Alex's troops are outnumbered, they win an incredible victory thanks to his strategic acumen. They advance and liberate the Greek cities along the coast of Asia Minor encountering very little resistance in the process.'

'You mean he conquered them?'

'Actually, he allowed them to choose the regime of their preference. Most were former democracies and they returned to that political system.'

'But wasn't Macedonia a kingdom? Why would they allow the establishment of democracies? What was in it for them? Shouldn't the king have assumed sovereignty over those cities?'

'It's an example of how Alexander stands out among leaders. In any case, he keeps going, making a pit-stop at Gordium, where he ingeniously cuts through the eponymous knot, and pushes forward towards Syria. There's another battle there, at Issus. This time Persia musters a truly astounding number of troops, but not only does Alex win, he causes the Persian king, Darius III, to flee the field mid-battle, leaving behind his mother, his wife, and all the royal trappings that he'd brought along on his campaign.

'Alex finally reaches Egypt, where he is hailed as a liberator because in advance of his arrival, the Persians, with whom the Egyptians had never been on the best of terms, had fled. The Egyptians fall all over themselves in adulation, "Alex, you're a superstar! No, you're a god!" It is at this point that Alex begins to take their words literally, and, it bears noting, he develops a real soft spot for Egypt. Of course, the Greeks had been familiar with Egyptian culture for centuries and many were real aficionados. Besides, Egyptian culture was a lot older than Greek. For instance, keep in mind that the Great Pyramid of Giza was more ancient to Alexander than he is to us today. On the edge of the Nile Delta, he founds one of the dozens of cities named after him, although this one is destined to become the most famous. In any case, he presses on with his campaign and finally makes his grand entrance into Asia. As he begins his advance on the beating heart of Persia, Darius, via courier, extends an offer: "How about we split the empire down the middle? You keep what you've conquered so far, and I keep the other half."'

'Not exactly a bad deal, was it?'

'One of Alex's greatest generals, the venerable Parmenion, was of the same opinion. He said, "If I were Alexander, I would accept this offer." Alex replied, "I too would accept, if I were Parmenion." Undeterred, Alex continues to advance and conquers the empire's many capital cities one by one. Triumphant, he enters Babylon, where we see the third and greatest battle of the campaign, at Gaugamela, which ends with Persia's definitive defeat. Alex is now leader of the Persian Empire.'

'That was it? Three battles?'

'For the conquest of the empire, yes. But it's not the end of Alex's legend by far, for he must now find Darius, who has been kidnapped for ransom by insurgents, and take him into custody. He makes it to the furthest reaches of the Persian Empire, and now in the environs of today's Pakistan he meets a local king, Porus, at the head of an enormous army with large troops of war elephants. Even though he, too, is vanquished by Alex at the Battle of Hydaspes, his prowess and courage impress the Macedonian leader, and having become fast friends, the latter makes his departure and allows Porus to remain in his position. This is when he must truly have started going off the deep end. But it was bound to happen, wasn't it? After all, he was young, handsome, successful, and both CEO and CFO of a family business that had literally conquered the world. Gripped by paranoia and fear, seeing enemies and conspiracies everywhere, he begins to have both collaborators and friends killed willy-nilly. Then, he suddenly takes deathly sick in Babylon.'

'With what?'

'We don't know. It's an enigma, one we've been trying to unravel for centuries.'

'I remember that after his death, his empire collapsed . . . Didn't he leave an heir?'

'In the delirium of the final hours before his death, he was asked who he named as heir and he mumbled, "the strongest one".'

'Nice one, Alexander! In Greece, everyone thinks they're the best and strongest.'

'Exactly! And so began an endless cycle of intrigue, sabotage, and mutual destruction among his generals that ended only when, several decades later, the decks had been cleared and the once vast empire had been definitively fragmented into smaller kingdoms.'

'Do you think that ultimately Alexander deserved his reputation?'

'The only figure in antiquity to become such an object of interest and inquiry is my man Alex. He is also unique in the fact that this interest comes from two opposing sides of the spectrum. On the one hand, there are those who only focus on his greatness and idolise him, as if he weren't a human being in possession of all the inevitable passions and weaknesses of the species. On the other hand, there are those who fall all over themselves to condemn him as a symbol of evil and imperialism, as the only leader to wage an expansionist war in ancient Greece. Oof, I tell you, I don't find this image of Alexander the Great, Slaughterer of Men, at all convincing! Hold on for just one sec, and think about it: Alex, a slaughterer? As opposed to whom? How do you think state differences were resolved before and after him? Through debate? As if other Greek politicians and generals – or politicians and military

leaders the world over throughout history, for that matter –
were all tree-hugging peaceniks! How do you think they won
their wars? By distributing petitions and collecting signa-
tures? Honestly, it makes no sense to compare Alexander with
Mahatma Ghandi. Besides, even if we cancel Alexander the
Great – off to the corner with you, naughty boy! – and condemn him for not being the philosopher saint that we wish
he were, does that mean that we have purged our history of
its least desirable aspects?'

'But he is the only conqueror in Greek history.'

'Whereas democratic Athens, which tormented its allies
and ran roughshod over the Aegean, was a paragon of peace
and civility! Do you know what they did to the island of Milos?
When Milos pleaded with Athens to be allowed to remain
neutral in the latter's conflicts with Sparta, Athens intentionally razed the island to the ground, slaughtered all the men,
and sold all the women and children into slavery. How's that
for conquest and bloodshed? What I'm trying to get at with
these rhetorical questions is why we need to distil Greek history into a false dichotomy of either victimhood or sainthood?
Why this need to whitewash history? Let's ask ourselves what
motivates this desire to pin on Alex alone all the violence and
fury that mars an idealised image of a glorious ancient Greece
floating in the heady clouds of philosophy, higher learning, and
beautiful art. Is it just to unwittingly champion a retrogressive
and covert nationalism? No, Alex the Great must be judged
as a leader in the context of world leaders, and when you do
that, he continues to come out on top. When we recognise and
condemn the fundamental role that violence has played in history as a whole the world over, we are better able to understand
the particularities of Alex's idiosyncratic and groundbreaking

influence in Greek affairs. Picking and choosing particular moments to condemn as if they didn't exist within this broader context makes no sense at all.'

'One final question: did he really civilise the barbarian hordes?'

'He didn't "civilise" anyone! He travelled through lands and encountered peoples whose civilisations had been around for millennia – certainly long before ancient Greece had come into being – and whose cultures had inspired the Greeks' while still in its infancy. Inevitably, however, his campaigns, which incidentally were accompanied by an entourage of scholars interested in studying these new places and cultures, disseminated some of the more appealing aspects of Greek culture: athleticism, the value of individuality, philosophy, literature, theatre, the branches of knowledge. In other words, his campaigns provided the opportunity for intercultural interaction and exchange between Greeks and other peoples that led to some truly dazzling outcomes. This type of cross-pollination, after all, is absolutely critical for culture, which cannot exist in a vacuum. Indeed, it needs exchange to both grow and thrive. Furthermore, despite his megalomania, Alex was smart enough to recognise that peaceful co-existence among different peoples depends on equal treatment. This is why he married off thousands of Greeks to foreign women. It's also why he quarrelled with his teacher, Aristotle. Aris did not agree with Alex's opinion that "barbarians" and Greeks ought to be considered equals.'

'Alexander quarrelled with Aristotle?'

'Well, it wasn't the only cause of their quarrel. There's the small fact that Alex killed Aris's nephew Callisthenes for suspicion of conspiring against him.'

'Ugh! You see! That's the kind of thing that tarnishes his myth.'

'But myths are just that: myths, not reality.'

'Since we're talking about myths, here's a random question that has been nagging at me for a while now, so I'm just going to ask it. Is it just me, or is mythology a big, convoluted jumble? And if so, why is it such a mess?'

FAQ

Why is Mythology Such a Mess?

'MYTHOLOGY IS INDEED A MESS. But it is only to be expected, because what we call mythology is, in essence, the stories that were used to embellish ancient Greek religion, and neither religion nor its accompanying mythologies were based on a single sacred text or figure, or even on the revelations of a single individual. In fact, there were no sacred texts in ancient Greece.'

'So how did the people know whom and how to worship?'

'Religious ideology and everything related to it was perpetuated through the oral tradition and passed on from one generation to the next. Since there was no dedicated sacred text for the religion, it stands to reason that there also wasn't a corresponding one for the mythology.'

'What, then, are our sources for the mythology?'

'To start, Homer and Hesiod, the first great epic poets of the eighth and seventh centuries BCE. Then came the various poets, including the tragic poets of the ancient theatre, who dipped liberally into the pool of mythology, adapting the stories they liked to heighten their drama and emotional resonance. In late antiquity, we see the advent of the novel, a genre that was particularly adept at playing to the tastes of its audience. Sprinkle this heady brew with the spice of local traditions, adaptations, and the wild joyrides of the human imagination, and we end up with a glorious miscellany of myths moulded primarily by the ingenuity of artistic creativity. In other words, what we know today as mythology is an assemblage of a host of different interpretations and variations that were embellished, adapted, re-embellished and so on and so forth endlessly. To this day there is no single version capacious enough to include the entire imaginative universe created by so many different minds over so many centuries. Perhaps this is why we continue to find Greek mythology so intriguing, so magnetic. It is not the product of a particular text, heaven-sent to tell us what's what.'

'I still want to know who created the myths.'

'The most creative minds of the period, the artists and thinkers; not the austere and inflexible wisdom of priests or dedicated holy men. Nurtured by the inspired imagination of artists, the myths are as expansive and flavourful as rising dough. You also mustn't forget that while mythology, for us, is simply a collection of great and entertaining stories, for the ancient Greeks it was part and parcel of their daily lives. Alexander the Great, for instance, really believed that he was a descendant of Heracles and a son of Zeus! Fat lot of good it does you when you die so young, you'll say, but if nothing else, his rival successors, also known as the *diadochi*, by the way, put this belief to good political use, which is why they were literally falling all over themselves to emulate him.'

'Ah, yes – tell me what happened after Alexander the Great's death.'

'Complete chaos. Listen to this . . .'

11

Big Old Changes
(The Hellenistic Period)

'WITH ALEXANDER'S DEATH came the virulent race for succession.'

'Were there any official heirs?'

'Yes and no. He had a son, Heracles, with his mistress Barsine, but the now-adolescent boy was not the fruit of a legitimate marriage.'

'Ah, I see, he was illegitimate. What about a legal heir?'

'Let's get one thing clear, even though it takes us off topic: there is no such thing as an illegitimate child, there are only illegitimate parents. In any case, yes, Alex had officially wed Roxana, princess of distant Bactria, reputedly the most beautiful woman he had ever seen. At the time of his death, Roxana was pregnant, but since they did not know if the child was a boy, it was unclear if they had a direct heir to the throne. In the meantime, Alex also had a half-brother, Arrhidaeus, Philip's son with a dancer, who seems to have had some disabilities of the intellectual variety. Long story short, Alex's generals and rival successors – utter vultures circling the skies in a bid to grab the biggest share of the empire if not the entire thing – decide to feign support for the claims to the throne of both his unborn child – who does turn out to be a boy and is named Alexander IV – and his disabled half-brother, Arrhidaeus, who is now renamed Philip III. Vowing to protect them, they install them both as king. This, my friend, opens the floodgates to whole-sale slaughter. For decades, Alexander's successors mobilised troops, changed alliances as if playing musical chairs, engaged in all manner of deception and treachery, married off their daughters and sons to those of their rivals, and, chiefly, sacrificed entire armies on the battlefield for personal gain.'

'And all this infighting splintered the empire? Into how many pieces?'

'Mainly, four larger pieces. The most significant kingdoms rising from this chaos were Ptolemy's, founder of the eponymous dynasty, which was based in Egypt, and Seleucus I Nicator's, who took over the largest portion of Asia and founded the Seleucid dynasty. He was the most tenacious about persevering with Alex's vision, but like the others, he too failed. The kingdom of Thrace's fortunes were not as promising as the other two, but it is during this period that we see a small kingdom in the north-western regions of Asia Minor begin to stir and, almost by accident, grow from a tiny city into a force to be reckoned with, both militaristically and culturally: the kingdom of Pergamon.'

'OK, but what happened to the kingdom of Macedonia?'

'It's a long story, so in a nutshell: Cassander, who was married to Alex's half-sister, Thessalonike, seized power. He founded and named two cities: Cassandreia, after himself, in the location where the city of Potidaea in Chalkidiki now stands, and Thessaloniki, after his wife. He clearly intended Cassandreia to become the most powerful city in Macedonia, but it didn't turn out that way. In fact, Thessaloniki became a lot larger and way more important. It has been a vibrant urban centre ever since. '

'And what about Alexander's legal heirs, his half-brother, and his son?'

'Philip Arrhidaeus was among the first to be cut down. As a matter of fact, he was put to death by Olympias, Alexander the Great's mother, to clear the way to the throne for her grandson, Alexander IV. You see, Alex's widow, Roxana, had sought refuge in Macedonia with her mother-in-law.'

'Olympias was that powerful?'

'Oh, she was a fearsome woman with a notoriously domineering personality. Nevertheless, she, her daughter-in-law, and grandson were all killed by Cassander. The story is that the soldiers he had originally instructed to kill Olympias chickened out, that's how terrifying she was. So Cassander, forced to find an alternative solution, had the brilliant idea of fighting fire with fire: he handed her over to the mothers and wives of those she had had killed. After they were done with her, they threw her body to the dogs.'

'Did they also throw little Alexander to the dogs?'

'Probably not. It is very likely that he was buried with all appropriate pomp and circumstance in keeping with his role as heir. It's thought that one of the royal tombs in the Great Tumulus at Aigai, excavated in the late 1970s, belongs to Alex's son, which is why we call it the "Prince's Tomb".'

'There was still one fairly close heir: the illegitimate son, Heracles, who you mentioned earlier.'

'Yes, he was still alive, and an adolescent at this point. In a brief crisis of conscience, one of the Macedonian generals, Polyperchon, thought to support his bid to the empty Macedonian throne. Cassander, however, soon put an end to that and convinced him that it was in everyone's interests for the royal family to be wiped from the face of the earth. That was the end of Heracles.'

'Did he too "go to the dogs"?'

'Good question. We don't know. But something did come to light recently that demonstrates how exhilarating archaeology can be. In 2008, during excavation of the Agora in the ancient city of Aigai, Macedonia's first capital city and the burial site of its kings, a hidden royal burial was found.'

'What do you mean "hidden"? How could it be both royal and hidden?'

'Even though it was tucked away in a metal vessel, the burial contained much evidence of the occupant's elite status, including a gold oak wreath. Gold wreaths were common grave goods in Macedonian elite tombs, and oak wreaths in particular, with their association to Zeus, are linked with the royal family, or at least to positions of very high prestige. The following year, in 2009, a similar burial was found close by. The bones in this second burial were in such poor condition that it was impossible to determine their age and sex. The bones in the first burial, though, were indicative of an adolescent male. It is not unreasonable, then, to conjecture that the burials might belong to the young Heracles and his mother, Barsine, both of whom were murdered. Perhaps a few remaining loyalists to the royal line, who admired Alexander and his legacy, had attempted to provide the honours befitting his last descendant and gave him a royal – albeit secret – burial. Naturally, we must be careful and refrain from saying that we've found Heracles's grave; we are justified in saying, though, that it looks somewhat likely.'

'So, after the death of Alexander the Great, in other words,

Macedonia is a royal mess and the rest of its empire has splintered into kingdoms. What's happening in the rest of Greece?'

'Various city-states tried to win their independence, but these were not hospitable times for such endeavours. The successors' enormous armies did not give them much room to manoeuvre, so the cities that were not drawn into the hungry maws of the rival successors' kingdoms formed *koina* – federated states of allyship, or leagues – so as to be better able to both defend themselves and fight back. The two largest leagues were the Achaean League in the Peloponnese and the Aetolian League in western Greece.'

'And did it work? Was there strength in allyship?'

'Both the Aetolians and the Achaeans became powers to be reckoned with, and they too lunged head-first into the unforgiving arena of war and conflict, shifting alliances and interests over the years, as if playing musical chairs.'

'May I ask something, even though I already asked the same question a little earlier, and I'm probably going to get the same answer? In all this chaos of war you're describing, was culture still able to evolve and thrive?'

'Yes, it was, my friend, because in one form or another, there was no end to war for the entire duration of antiquity. Keep in mind that we haven't come close to touching on all the wars and conflicts – I mean, how many can one stomach talking about? – and even as researchers we don't know the extent of it. They were endless, a part of life, just like there was no end to disease, the high mortality rate, the short life expectancy, the expendability of human life, and so on and so forth. Human beings, adaptable and restless at heart, have always managed to persevere through the fire and brimstone, and create culture.'

'You mean to say that Greek culture continues as we know it from the Classical period?'

'In the Hellenistic period, the Greek way of life spread through the entire world as understood by western humanity at the time, and these new circumstances also brought about new forms of stimulation. Indeed, the Hellenistic period's greatest cultural accomplishment barely needs introduction: wreathed in mythic splendour as the repository of all the greatest mysteries and knowledge of the ancient world (and I wouldn't say that this is too far from the truth), it is something we continue to study, and whose absence we regret. I am referring to the Museum (or Mouseion) of Alexandria.'

'Alexandria in Egypt?'

'Of course! One of the most important, if not *the* most important city of the Hellenistic period. Keep in mind that its harbour was the largest in the ancient world – that should give you a sense of the scale we're talking about.'

'The largest? You mean in terms of traffic and trade?'

'Size, too! Here's an illustrative example: Hiero II, the tyrant of Syracuse, another powerful Greek city in Sicily, built the largest ship the world had seen at the time, using sixty times the amount of timber needed for a regular ship, and with top-quality materials imported from far-flung regions: Spanish rope, French pitch, etc. He also enlisted Archimedes, the period's greatest mind, as chief engineer. The ship was built to accommodate twenty rows of oars and three decks. The lower or hold deck was used for the transportation of cargo and also contained the servants' quarters, as well as storage rooms, stables, ovens, carpentry workshops, mills, and even an aquarium. The main living quarters, thirty rooms with four beds each, were located on the middle deck, along with a gymnasium, gardens, and a temple to Aphrodite. The top deck featured all sorts of defensive and military weaponry – catapults, crossbows . . . it was, in short, an entire self-sufficient floating city, capable of feeding and supporting, entertaining and defending itself. It was known as the Syracusia.'

'It must have caused quite the sensation!'

'More like a sensational failure! You see, it was too big to port anywhere, except for Alexandria. The ship only sailed once, when poor Hiero was forced to send it as a gift to Egypt, where we think it was kept in Alexandria's harbour as a floating mall.'

'Wow! Alexandria sounds really impressive. You said that they had a museum? With exhibits?'

'No, not that kind of museum, not like the ones we're familiar with today. The Mouseion in Alexandria was like a research centre for higher learning. It was called Mouseion because it was dedicated to the Muses, those nine young goddesses of literature, science, and the arts, and the daughters of Zeus and Mnemosyne, or power and memory. Naturally, the Mouseion needed texts. And where were the texts kept? In Alexandria's famous library.'

'What made them build the library?'

'Ptolemy, one of Alex the Great's generals, friends, and classmates at Aristotle's school, was a highly educated man whose love of literature and the arts led him to do something utterly unique in the annals of history: he founded the Mouseion, a space for thinking and research, and invited the participation of the greatest minds of the time. He promised them the moon and stars, and actually kept his word. All the great thinkers who flocked to Alexandria were given room and board, a decent income, extra funding for any research they wished to conduct, tax exemption – you name it, they got it; he catered to their every whim, as long as they did the work! Naturally, to nurture the work and better bring it to fruition, Ptolemy decided to provide access to as much pre-existing knowledge as possible. Not only did he go about collecting it, but he had it studied, analysed, corrected, corroborated. In short, he set up a system for its formal classification, systematisation, and expansion. The Alexandria Library came to contain the largest number of texts ever collected in the ancient world.'

'How did they find and collect so many texts? I imagine that in a period without printing presses, originals were rare and copies even rarer.'

'First, they confiscated any circulating texts that they could easily lay their hands on. Second, they unleashed a veritable army to hunt down manuscripts and books by hook or by crook, and they succeeded in collecting every scrap of textual material throughout the entire Mediterranean. A good example is what happened in Athens, where they went in search of the manuscripts by the great tragic poets: Aeschylus, Sophocles, and Euripides. Naturally, the Athenians wouldn't dream of parting with them, so the Alexandrians proposed to borrow, copy, and return them, and offered a deposit of fifteen talents as a guarantee.'

'Was it a large sum?'

'It was an enormous sum. One talent was more than enough to cover a month's wages for not one but an entire crew of a military trireme! Given the size of the security, the Athenians took the Alexandrians at their word, but what actually happened is that once the manuscripts were in Alexandria, the copies, not the originals, were sent back to Athens. The Alexandrians didn't care about losing the deposit; all they cared about was collecting the texts.'

'That library must have been truly impressive, eh?'

'Unfortunately, we don't have much information about the library. We don't even know what it looked like. As a rule of thumb, though, don't go picturing ancient libraries like those of today. The main reason is that they didn't contain books, but cylinders with scrolls of papyri. We do know, of course, as I've already mentioned, that all, or almost all, ancient knowledge was collected, studied, recorded, analysed, and preserved there. Alexandria thus became the de facto cultural centre of the Hellenistic period. But it wasn't the only such centre, and soon it gained quite a formidable cultural rival. A small city in north-western Asia Minor, Pergamon, was becoming the capital of a very powerful and wealthy Hellenistic kingdom. Envious of Alexandria's renown, Pergamon proceeded to build a library and focus its energies on cultural development. Attempting to quash the rivalry once and for all, Egypt reputedly prohibited the export of papyrus to Pergamon.'

'So what – wasn't it available anywhere else?'

'Actually, no. Even though the use of papyrus as a writing surface was widespread throughout the Mediterranean, Egypt had the monopoly on its production. Undeterred, though, Pergamon began producing in bulk an existing but hitherto not very popular writing material made from specially pre-pared untanned leather. Soon all the rage as the new, chic way to write, this material became known as parchment. Perga-mon, however, did not stop there: it became a pioneer in the arts, and was soon renowned for its particularly ornate style. How ornate, you ask? A lot – so much so that its style was called the Pergamene Baroque. In sculpture, groups of figures arranged either in clusters or in a line, assumed a new importance.'

'What's the difference?'

'Well, the clustered statues are dynamically intertwined, like in the world-famous Laocoön Group statue, whereas the "in line" groups stand next to each other as if at a line-up, like the ex-voto of Daochos at Delphi.'

'So I guess sculpture changes a lot in that period?'

'Yes, sculpture really soars, and there are some truly stunning examples. There's the monumental Pergamon Altar, now kept at the Pergamon Museum in Berlin, with its hundreds of enormous statues of the gods and Titans embroiled in battle; there's the glorious Winged Victory of Samothrace, now found in the Louvre in Paris, poised for landing as the wind plasters her tunic's folds of fabric against her body.'

'What about ceramics? Are the Athenian black-figure and red-figure vases still being made?'

'Look, as I've mentioned, humans never stopped producing clay vessels throughout their history. What does change in this period, though, is that the black-figure and red-figure styles that were once in such demand throughout the Mediterranean go out of style, and we see the development of different ceramic idioms.'

'That's how it's always been. Fashions come and go.'

'Indeed. Monochrome vessels now take centre stage – some in red, but mainly in black, adorned with such simple and discreet patterns they look like embroidery. We call this style West Slope Ware.'

'What kind of name is that?'

'The name comes from the fact that the first vessels of this type were found on the west slope of the Acropolis. Which is also where the King of Pergamon had the Stoa of Eumenes built as a gift to Athens.'

'Wait – what's a Stoa?'

'A Stoa is an elongated colonnaded structure.'

'So how did we get from ceramics to a Stoa?'

'Because we were talking about kings of the Hellenistic period, and I brought up the Acropolis.'

'Why did the king donate a colonnade?'

'Colonnaded buildings, the Stoas, are among ancient Greece's most significant architectural achievements, and – guess what? – they become a hot commodity in the Hellenistic period. In fact, they're being built everywhere. The simplicity of their design is truly remarkable. In essence, we're talking about a roofed corridor, with room for many possible uses – from storage space to shops, archives, restaurants, and anything else you can imagine – closed on one side, and on the other supported by open columns that permit the entry of plenty of light and air. The closed side was always situated facing north, to provide shelter from the winter cold and the northerly winds. The open, south-facing side allowed entry to the low and warming winter sun, but barred the high summer sun's rays, thus ensuring that the space remained cool.'

'Is that where philosophers would hang out and chew the fat?'

'Yes, but colonnades were also used more generally. Of course, during the Hellenistic period, public philosophical discussions at the Stoa must have been a common sight because there's a tremendous flourishing of philosophical activity at this time. Hordes of new philosophers either built on the work of the previous, Classical generation, or they founded their own systems of thought. This is when we see the rise of Epicureanism, Stoicism, and other schools.'

'Uh-oh – a rat's nest!'

'Greece's flourishing culture drew the attention of a small city in central Italy that was in the process of amassing the power required to change the entire world. Rome at that time was not particularly remarkable. But this is when it began to communicate and become truly enthralled with Greek culture.'

'How did it go from being a small city, as you call it, to conquering the world?'

'Determination, brio, and the fact that it came in contact with other, already advanced cultures. Rome had two great adversaries standing in her way for dominion over the Mediterranean. The Carthaginians to the west and the Greeks to the east, both of whom invaded Italy. On the Greek side it was Pyrrhus, the King of Epirus, a cousin of Alexander the Great, who is considered one of the greatest generals of antiquity.'

'Was Epirus a powerful kingdom?'

'Very much so. They were governed by the Molossian ruling dynasty.'

'They were named after the Molossus breed of dog?'

'The other way around! The dog is an Epirote breed and so was named after the dynasty. As I was saying, Epirus had a really powerful dynasty. In fact Olympias, wife of Philip II of Macedon and Alex's mum, was a Molossian princess.'

'Oh, so Alexander the Great was half Epirote?'

'Yes, and the Epirotes were extremely proud of the fact. Pyrrhus, in particular, kept vacillating between awe and envy for his famous cousin, which is probably what inspired him to play the conqueror too. He entered Italy, yet despite repeated wins in battle, he also sustained catastrophic losses. This is where the phrase "Pyrrhic victory" comes from. A victory, in other words, that comes to nothing, because you've sacrificed so much to achieve it.'

'But since they were losing, didn't the Romans sustain catastrophic losses too?'

'Of course they did. But the Romans had something that Pyrrhus lacked: reserves. They could easily marshal a new army, while Pyrrhus was obliged to fight with the rapidly dwindling number of troops he had brought to the Italian Peninsula. The defeat of Rome's other great rival, Carthage, can be traced to the same cause.'

'Can you tell me a little about Carthage?'

'Carthage was the largest Phoenician city in the western Mediterranean. Extremely ancient, it had initially been a Phoenician colony on the coast of Africa, but soon became so powerful that it cut ties to its founding metropolis and became one in its own right, seeding colonies throughout the western Mediterranean. It was a longstanding rival of the Greek colonies in the region and later, of course, with Rome. Indeed, Rome was almost brought to its knees by Hannibal.'

'Who was this Hannibal?'

'Hannibal of Carthage was a legendary general who took the war to the Romans' doorstep. He marched through all of today's Spain and southern France, crossed the Alps with war elephants, and repeatedly beat the Romans on the battlefield.'

'How did he manage that?'

'The fellow was undoubtedly a military genius. He played with the Roman legions like a cat does with a mouse. But, as I've already mentioned, the Romans had something he didn't: reserves.'

'The Romans prevailed on their home ground?'

'Not only did they eventually prevail, but, riled up as they were, they decided to hit back. It was now time for their counter-attack. First, they turned to Carthage. Because the

Greeks too had settled parts of the western Mediterranean and they weren't on the best of terms with the Carthaginians, the Romans used the Greeks against the Carthaginians and the Carthaginians against the Greeks. Their gambit worked. In the eastern Mediterranean, where there was no Carthaginian presence, Rome turned the Greeks against themselves, and again they were successful.'

'Carthage was only one city, while the Hellenistic kingdoms and states were quite numerous. Didn't the sheer number of Greek states raise some difficulties for the Romans?'

'But it didn't tangle with them all at once! First, it set its sights on Macedonia. With all the military power at its disposal, as well as the aid of Greeks from the south, it vanquished Perseus, the last king of Macedon, who was taken captive to Rome. This was in 168 BCE, at the Battle of Pydna.'

'What about the rest of Greece?'

'Twenty years later, the Romans would win their definitive victory over that, too, the most significant milestone being the total destruction of Corinth in 148 BCE. Not that other cities were spared the Roman ire. General Sulla, for example, showed no leniency when he finally entered besieged Athens. Prior to his advance, an Athenian delegation was sent to attempt to dissuade him. They took a tack that had proved successful in the past when other invading generals had spared the city because of their affection for Greek culture. Attempting to tug on his heartstrings, the delegation proceeded to expound on the glorious history of Athens and the wonders of its cultural accomplishments, to no avail. Sulla was cut of a different cloth than his predecessors. He replied: "What is it to me that you were once the cradle of culture. I did not come here to be given lessons. I came to bring the rebels to heel." Athens was summarily sacked and burned and thousands of works of art were plundered and taken to Rome. Naturally, Athens's ruin served as a warning to other Greek city-states.'

'Were there any independent Greek states left?'

'All were conquered in one way or another. Across the Aegean, in Asia Minor, the wealthy and powerful Hellenistic kingdom of Pergamon was bequeathed to Rome.'

'What do you mean, "bequeathed"? By whom? How? In a will? You mean to say that the king wrote "my kingdom goes to Rome" in his will?' He laughed at the absurdity of this scenario.

'Don't laugh, my friend, because that's exactly what happened.'

He stopped mid-laugh, his eyes almost popping out of his head.

'The last king of Pergamon literally left his kingdom to the Romans. It was, in fact, stipulated in his will. The Pergamon citizenry protested in vain since, obviously, Rome made no bones about claiming its inheritance. Later they conquered the Seleucid Empire and all other outlying areas of resistance, and were left with the last-standing Hellenistic kingdom in history, Ptolemaic Egypt, which did give them a run for their money, truth be told. The legendary Cleopatra was the last queen to sit on its throne, and, as we know, Julius Caesar, who had gone to negotiate with her, ended up falling head over heels. Caesar, however, a dictator who had presided over a great concentration of power under his regime, was soon assassinated.'

'Dictator? You mean emperor, don't you?'

'That's a common misconception. Julius Caesar was never emperor of Rome. The Roman Empire as a political entity was founded after his death. Up to that point, Rome was governed by a *res publica,* or elected oligarchy. *Res* meaning "affairs" and *publica* meaning "public": public affairs.'

'Is that where the term "republic" comes from?'

'Yes, and to this day, as evidenced in the United States, it's a system that is fundamentally more conservative in practice and ethos than democracy.'

'When did the Roman Republic end?'

'Shortly after Caesar's death. Before the establishment of the Empire, and after the death of Caesar who had fallen for Cleopatra, however, another important Roman, General Marcus Antonius, commonly known as Mark Antony, travelled to Alexandria, and guess what? He too fell in love with Cleopatra.'

'Quite the siren, wasn't she?'

'Oh, yes, she was a killer queen, guaranteed to blow your mind and so on and so forth! All joking aside, though, she was known as a femme fatale even back then. But the downside was that she did not have the best of reputations. Antonius had a rival, Octavian, who did not lose the opportunity to rally popular sentiment against him. Rome's conservative society took Octavian's side: Antonius had lost his head and run straight into the claws of a conniving witch! The Romans weren't born yesterday; they knew what those foreign women were capable of, and they wouldn't stand for it! A civil war broke out which was essentially a war waged by Rome against Egypt, because Antonius fought on Cleopatra's side, or perhaps it was the other way around . . . in any case, Octavian's troops clashed with Antonius's and Cleopatra's at the Battle of Actium in the southern part of Epirus by the Ionian Sea, and the definitive victory went to Octavian. At this point, Antonius and Cleopatra committed suicide. Rome was now mistress of the Mediterranean, and Octavian, gripped by the spirit of the new era, changed his name to Caesar Augustus and became the first Roman emperor.'

'That was the beginning of the Roman Empire? The notorious empire of intrigue, treachery, and debauchery?' He smirked.

'That's a very high opinion you have of the Roman Empire!'

'It was quite sketchy and seedy, wasn't it? A bit of a dark time.'

'Well, my friend, all of antiquity had a dark side to it. I mean, look here . . .'

FAQ

Was There a Dark Side to Antiquity?

'WE ARE ACCUSTOMED TO thinking of classical antiquity as purely admirable. And, of course, it is admirable, but that doesn't mean that's all there is to it. If you really want to get to know antiquity, you must also grapple with its less admirable aspects.'

'Aren't you just bursting the bubble when you do that?'

'What's wrong with that? I've said it before, and I'll say it again: history is neither simple nor monolithic, and confronting the darker aspects of the classical past shouldn't erase the reasons for our admiration of its glories. At the same time, we can't and shouldn't ignore the darkness: in fact, if we really want to understand the past, it is essential that we confront its less familiar underside, rejoice in the fact that humanity has progressed in various ways, and retain an understanding of the inevitability of this combination of light and dark in everything.'

'Alright, then, give me a specific example of this "darkness" in Greek antiquity.'

'For one, there was no compassion for human frailty. Disability, whether congenital or acquired, was practically a condemnation. Remember our conversation about Phryne and how physical beauty was revered as a favour from the gods? Well, if the opposite were true—'

'You were worthless.'

'The idea that support might be put in place to help the disabled, that their lives might be improved – these were completely foreign concepts. Many of the babies born with some perceived "abnormality" were abandoned in the wild to die alone.'

'You mean like at Kaiadas Cave, the Spartan pit of death?'

'Actually, that is a misconception: Kaiadas Cave was used for criminals, not children. It is true, however, that disabled children were sometimes abandoned to die, but not only in Sparta – it was general practice throughout Greece. Babies born with a "defect", who either looked disfigured or were otherwise simply unwanted, were often left on the side of a mountain to be torn apart by wild beasts. Have you heard of the mythical hero, Oedipus? Where do you think his name, which means "swollen-foot", came from? From the fact that his father, the King of Thebes, fearful of the prophesy that predicted his death by his son's hand, bored two holes through the heels of the infant's feet, in order to string him up to a tree and leave him to die. The swelling, or oedema, in Oedipus's feet was a lifelong reminder of this brutal treatment. In all likelihood, most babies left out to die were not boys but girls, because women did not have equal rights at the time, depending when and where in

Greece, of course. We can't overgeneralise and assume that this applied everywhere and always throughout antiquity, for that too is incorrect. Generally, though, in most of the ancient world during Greece's Classical period, women – a good fifty per cent of the population – were deprived of basic human rights that most of us today thankfully take for granted, thanks to protracted struggle and hard-won victories by many generations of activists.'

'But ancient Greeks worshipped both gods and goddesses, and in myth, women were not inferior to the male characters.'

'True ... OK, I take your point about egalitarianism among the gods. When it comes to human characters in myth, however, the situation is more complicated. Let's take a closer look at a constellation of myths that are obviously the products of the male imagination and disseminate a rather disturbing image of women. Princess Medea is the first case in point: daughter of King Aeëtes of distant Colchis, she decides to run off with Jason, who had arrived out of the blue with an entire ship full of Argonauts to steal nothing less than the golden fleece. And OK, fair enough, let's say that Medea's father, Aeëtes, is both a bad man and a cruel king with a criminal record crammed full of dastardly deeds that partially justifies the punishment that befalls him. The thing is, though, that Medea does not inflict this punishment directly – oh, no. Instead, when she flees with Jason, she takes her young brother, Absyrtus, with her, and as Aeëtes and his ships threaten to overtake them, she cuts the boy's body into pieces and tosses them one by one into the sea! In stopping to gather his son's limbs, Aeëtes is delayed, which gives the Argonauts the opportunity to get away. When Medea and Jason's relationship sours, she slaughters the children they had together and disappears. Female nature is portrayed as unimaginably savage and vengeful, while the men are presented as honourable victims.'

'Yeah, but that's just one particular myth!'

'No, it's not the only one. The myth of the two sisters, Procne and Philomela, ends similarly. The King of Thrace, Tereus, marries Procne and they have a son, Itys. After Tereus rapes Procne's sister, Philomela, the sisters get their revenge by murdering the young Itys and running off. The myth of Aëdon and Chelidon is very similar, except that the names are different.'

'Wow! All these stories of violent women!'

'Exactly! Did you notice how, in all these myths, women are depicted as lacking any maternal instincts whatsoever? In a patriarchal world, the destruction of the male heir is a father's worst possible punishment, and maternal – or more generally female – nature is presented as bloodthirsty and empty of feeling. There is only one mother in the annals of mythology who dares protest her daughter's sacrifice and resist the murderous father: Clytemnestra. She does not condone Agamemnon's decision to sacrifice their daughter, Iphigenia, on the altar of the Trojan War. She too, however, is ultimately denounced as a bad wife for taking a lover during her husband's ten-year sabbatical dedicated to war and pillaging. Clearly, all the mythical characters I've just mentioned do not present women in a particularly positive light. It's also true, though, that not all women in myth are paranoid infanticides. In any case, it's high time we came to terms with the way certain myths reinforced and perpetuated some of patriarchal ideology's most blatant prejudices.'

'Yes, OK, I see that. I guess I had never thought of it that way. Besides these feminist concerns, though, what else was problematic about ancient Greek culture?'

'Women and the disabled were not the only ones to experience injustice in antiquity. If you happened to be born a slave, life could be a real torment, even though it really varied from case to case. House slaves who were treated as an integral part of a wealthy urban household were literally worlds apart from slaves assigned to digging in a mine, for example. The latter's untimely deaths due to the exceptionally harsh conditions would have been nothing more than a nuisance to the overseers charged with offloading the bodies. Slaves in the first scenario, however, in all likelihood had a better quality of life than free but poverty-stricken citizens. Furthermore, it was common practice to either give slaves the opportunity to buy their freedom, or have it bestowed on them as a favour.'

'But wasn't slavery for life? You could get out of it?'

'It was not uncommon for slave owners to issue written attestations that were then shared publicly in one of the divine sanctuaries (the equivalent to signing a legally binding contract) in which they declared that at their death, a particular slave would be granted his or her freedom and nothing was to stand in their way. Slaves were also often paid salaries that they then used to buy their own freedom. In some very rare instances, slaves and masters developed strong emotional bonds. This was the case with a slave woman whose name, Aischre, means shameful or despicable. Quite the moniker, eh? Because she was a slave from Phrygia, it was, in all probability, the result of a renaming that denoted her fallen status. Aischre, then, served as wet nurse and nursemaid to a baby boy, Mikko, who, once grown to adulthood, began to take care of the now elderly woman. When she died, he erected a monument to her memory with the following epigraph: "Mikko took care of Aischre from Phrygia all her life. Let this monument serve as a reminder to the following generations. For the generous gift of milk from her breast, she received her reward in her dotage."

'Oh, come on, stop – you're going to make me cry!'

'I close with a rhetorical question: who do you think had a better quality of life? The trusted house slave in the upper echelons of the Roman Empire, or the free labourer living in absolute squalor in a tiny hovel with his large family?'

'Are you implying that it was better to be a slave?'

'Not even close. It's undeniable that slavery was a terrible institution. At this moment in time in particular, we can't imagine being denied our freedom – it is a cornerstone of our existence, of our notion of self and individuality. This is why there were, and indeed continue to be, protracted struggles throughout the world for the abolishment of slavery. At the same time, we also need to acknowledge that the dichotomy of slavery versus freedom can be a little too pat and simplistic. The status of freedom under the law, for example, all too often does not guarantee a basic quality of life. Correspondingly, in the period we are discussing, it was not uncommon to go from being free to becoming a slave, only to then eventually regain one's freedom. Transitions in social standing, either upward or downward, were a fact of life. Many of the Greeks who achieved renown and success in Rome during the period when it governed almost the entire western world, for example, were the slaves of wealthy Romans who had them tutor their children. Every Roman family with an ounce of self-respect, you see, was required to speak Greek and learn about Greek culture.'

'Why?'

'Because during the Roman period we see a marriage of cultures between Greece and Rome that is truly unparalleled in global history.'

'Wow! That's impressive.'

'Yes, it certainly is . . . and we haven't even scratched the surface yet . . .'

12

Kill Me Softly
(The Roman Period)

'WELCOME TO THE ROMAN PERIOD! This once small city now holds the reins not only to the entire Mediterranean but far beyond, stretching all the way from cloudy Britain's damp fields to the hot, sandy dunes of northern Africa and Arabia. Most of the Greek world is now encompassed in a handful of central provinces within this enormous empire; provinces that are both central and peaceful, because Greece hits it off with Rome, and Rome, in turn, thinks the world of Greece. Greece and Rome's relations have been the focus of much historical research, and the prevailing view is that they are truly unique in world history.'

'What was so unique about them?'

'The fact that after many years of military conflict, the Greeks and the Romans, who shared many similarities but also significant differences, actually end up getting along. It wouldn't be a stretch to say that they fall in love, and head over heels for that matter. From the moment they first set eyes on each other, the Greeks are awed by Rome's discipline, resourcefulness, and decisiveness, while the Romans are irresistibly drawn to Greece's intellectual and artistic sensibilities. Indeed, the

Romans become so enamoured of Greek culture that they do everything in their power to convince themselves and everyone else that they share the same heritage. Homer and the Trojan Wars in particular provide the grounds for this claim, and the Romans convince themselves that they are descendants of Aphrodite.'

'What? How?'

'According to legend, the goddess Aphrodite fell in love with Anchises, a Trojan, with whom she had a son, Aeneas, who fought in the Trojan War. When Troy fell, this Aeneas hoisted his elderly father on his shoulders, took his one and only son, Ascanius, by the hand, bundled them on a ship, and they all fled to escape the slaughter. After protracted wanderings that recall Odysseus's, Aeneas ended up in central Italy, where his descendants, Romulus and Remus, or Romos, built the city of Rome. By extension, then, Aphrodite becomes widely identified as the mother of the Roman state, and Rome gains its own resident epic hero.'

'This is all in Homer?'

'No, this is in Virgil, the greatest epic poet of Rome's golden epoch, who, wishing to emulate Homer and the success of the *Odyssey* and the *Iliad* , wrote the *Aeneid*.'

'Wow! The Romans were really eager to identify with the Greeks, weren't they?'

'Yes, because they were completely gaga about the culture. As descendants of Aphrodite and great-grandchildren of the Homeric heroes, the Romans laid claim to a piece of the Greek legacy. They were even allowed to participate in the Panhellenic Games, as if they were distant cousins of sorts, even if only by marriage. They also spoke excellent Greek, and they liked traveling to Greece and admiring its ancient cities, to the point that

Roman Hellenomania became the hottest new trend. It was also inevitable, then, that the Romans would fall in love with Greek art.'

'Do you mean that they began to copy Greek art?'

'Not just that. They wanted to get their hands on the originals, too. An endless number of ships with holds full of Greek art began to set sail from Greek harbours with Rome as their final destination. Some never got there. Most likely, one such ill-fated ship was the infamous Antikythera wreck, where the Antikythera mechanism was found.'

'What was that?'

'A very complicated mechanism that was used to calculate and measure planetary and celestial movements. The probable accident that claimed the ship and the lives of its crew and passengers preserved it for us. Having run into a raging storm, the ship capsized and sank, and it wasn't until centuries later that the beautiful statues in its hold came to light. Most of them, the ones that were not buried in the sandy seabed, were destroyed by the water and its peculiar inhabitants. Generally, the deeper a shipwreck sinks, the better preserved the relics, because the closer they are to the surface the more turbulent the sea and the stronger its tides.'

'OK, so the Romans fell in love – but it sounds like all they did was take, take, take. Did they give anything at all?'

'They certainly did. First off, the Romans gave the Greeks something that they had been incapable of giving themselves: peace. The Pax Romana, which means Roman Peace in Latin, has become legendary. They also built a superior road network. The best that the ancient Greeks had been able to come up with in regards to a road system was to create two furrows in the earth or rock for the wheels of their carts.'

'How did they know how wide to make the furrows?'

'Other way around, my friend! They designed their carts to fit the width of the furrows. The Romans, however, had discovered how to pave their roads. What kinds of roads, you ask? Roads the likes of which had never been seen before! Wide boulevards that went straight through tall mountains, swampy plains, rivers and valleys, and took you from one corner of the empire to the other. Ah, also, all roads led to Rome. In general, they made travel a lot safer.'

'Why wasn't it safe to travel?'

'In Greek antiquity, roads were not managed or supervised by a state power. City-states were only concerned with what went on within their borders. Therefore, travellers were entirely at the mercy of nature and the various crooks and bandits lurking there. This is another reason why people mainly travelled by ship in antiquity. It was faster and slightly – only slightly – more reliable.'

'Why only slightly?'

'Because, as I've mentioned several times, our ancestors were quite superstitious. Keep in mind that ships back then were nothing like the ferry boats of today. They were either fishing boats or military and merchant ships, and of the three, only the last kind accommodated the general public. This is how it worked: you'd go down to the harbour and wait for a ship headed in the direction of the destination that you wanted to get to. Then, you'd pay your fare, but that was far from the end of it, because if someone happened to sneeze as they climbed on board, it was taken as a bad omen, and the ship would stay put. If a black bird happened to alight on the stays – oops, bad omen! – the ship remained where it was. If one of the passengers had a bad dream the night before the ship was due to sail

– uh-oh, bad omen again! – you weren't going anywhere. In short, if the sacrifice, or this, that, and the other had not gone well, the ship's anchor would not budge. If, after all this, all signs were finally auspicious, or at least not full of gloom and doom, you had to wait for a favourable wind. And as if all this weren't enough, there was also always the possibility of piracy, which fortunately decreased considerably under the Roman Empire.'

'It sounds like the Romans really did some good.'

'Yes, they certainly did. They also provided a new range of architectural structures that led to more practical and functional building projects: aqueducts, residential housing blocks, public baths and toilets, sewer systems . . . in general, they really raised the standard of living. They changed many, many things. Just as the Greeks had been inspired by eastern culture centuries earlier and made it theirs by building and "improving" on it, so the Romans were inspired by the Greeks to build something all their own. The fundamental difference between the Greek and Roman approach is in the scale. The Greeks, for example, already had baths, and so the Romans built dozens of baths in their capital. The difference is that while Greek baths were small and functional, the inhabitants of Rome during the golden years of empire could choose among enormous bath complexes filled with statues and works of art, spaces for entertainment, and even specialised libraries dedicated to the bathers' spiritual and intellectual uplift.'

'But weren't the Romans using Greek architectural models for their building?'

'Yes, the architecture is very similar. But in contrast to the Greeks, who were partial to the Doric and Ionic orders, the Romans preferred the Corinthian. In fact, wherever you see Corinthian capitals, whether in Greece or throughout the Mediterranean, you are most likely looking at something that was built during the Roman Empire. For example, the columns of the Temple of Olympian Zeus. Also, the thin red bricks you see in some ancient walls, that's a Roman building technique. Some of the best examples are in Thessaloniki and Nicopolis in the region of Preveza.'

'Are you saying that Nicopolis and Thessaloniki are Roman cities?'

'Thessaloniki existed already, but Nicopolis was founded during the Roman period. Both, however, are brimming with antiquities from the era. For convenience's sake, we call them Roman, but they could just as easily have been built by Greeks during this time. Let's take the Odeon of Herodes Atticus under the Acropolis as an example. Officially, it's a Roman building, but it was actually built by an obscenely wealthy Athenian, Herodes Atticus.'

'A big spender, eh?'

'He built it to blow smoke up their you-know-whats, my friend! You see, he had some pretty major skeletons in his closet due to the death of his pregnant wife, Regilla.'

'He killed her?'

'He got his slave to kick her in the belly, and both she and the baby died. The wife's family, who had been against the marriage from the very beginning, dragged him through the courts. Herodes happened to be a good friend of the emperor's so he got off scot-free, but to appease the wrath of public opinion and assume the persona of grieving widower, he built the Odeon Theatre in his wife's memory. It should be noted, too, though, that he was a big supporter of the arts in general, and, at the time, art was still a big commodity.'

'But you said that the Romans copied much of Greek art.'

'Yes, it's true that in the arts they mimicked the Greek styles they admired, but they also gave us something completely new: the portrait. Greeks preferred their representations of the human body in perfect and idealised form. The Romans, by contrast, were all about realism. No matter how saggy and wrinkled the senator, or how plain-looking the noblewoman, they wanted to see themselves mirrored in the sculpture. Their general attitude was: "I'm paying, so I'm the boss, and I certainly don't want to see any old generic face in place of mine. I want to see myself!"'

'How did the Greeks react to this coexistence?'

'It seems that they took to it. It's notable that for the centuries of Roman occupation, there were no Greek revolts or independence movements. In fact, the Greeks became so used to the Roman status quo that they didn't do anything to change it. Why would they? Peace and prosperity prevailed, Greek art and ways of life were not only accepted but celebrated, and Greek was now an international language – throughout the eastern part of the empire, at least. In fact, as attested to by the literature of the time, scholars and thinkers from other parts of the world were beginning to write in Greek.'

'Give me an example.'

'Lucian was a Syrian from Samosata. He was apprenticed to become a sculptor, but was so useless at it that his uncle, who owned the workshop, kicked him out. He got hooked on education, learned Greek better even than his mother tongue, studied, and found his ikigai. His imagination was boundless!'

'You mean for the time?'

'For ours too. He's the author of *A True Story*, which brutally satirises past and contemporaneous writers of fantastical tales full of imaginary and exotic places and peoples. It was the first sci-fi novel ever written. His protagonist first wanders the entire globe and then travels to the moon, where he discovers that the Moon King is actually an earthling who was kidnapped by aliens. He learns that the inhabitants of the moon, having established a colony on Aphrodite's planet, Venus, are under attack by the Sun King. Saddled on giant beetles, bumble bees, and other types of insects, the two armies are fighting it out.'

'You must be joking! Why haven't they made a movie of it yet?'

'Oh, you don't know the half of it yet! In *Trial in the Court of Vowels*, the letter "s" accuses the letter "t" of stealing words from him and takes him to court. The vowels sit in judgement.'

'How on earth was "t" stealing words?'

'Haven't you heard of the famous cry "*Thalatta, Thalatta*", meaning "the sea, the sea" that was uttered by the roaming ten thousand Greeks when they finally saw water after their failed expedition against the Persians? Well, the joke is that the double "t"s in "*thalatta*" are occupying the place of the later double "s"s that we see in the more modern versions of the word "*thalassa*". Anyway, Luke was just full of such witticisms. In *The Mimes of the Courtesans* he describes amusing scenes from the lives of courtesans in antiquity, and in *The Gods in Council* he describes a ludicrous conversation among the twelve gods who have gathered to air concerns about the opening up of the Greek world and the threat to their livelihood posed by the arrival of foreign gods. They fear a deficiency in supplies of nectar and ambrosia, and they accuse Dionysus of having brought Pan into their midst, whose goatlike features debase the good looks and elegance associated with their class. To round things up, they also accuse Apollo of greedily hogging too many professions. He is, after all, god of music, medicine, and divination.'

'They have a point!'

'Finally, they decide to put together a seven-member Commission of Inquiry to examine the legitimacy of each god's claim to divinity.'

'Good for Luke! Lucky Luke. Why were we never taught any of this?'

'Well, you're hearing about it now.'

'But it's not the same now.'

'Why not? Learning is about acquiring information and combining it in new ways, isn't it? Does it really matter where you do that learning? What's most important is that you assimilate and use it.'

'Yes, you're right. Anyway, I can't resist asking, even though you may find the question annoying: since the Roman Empire was so powerful and prosperous, how and why did it fall?'

'Remember how I said that there were many and complicated reasons for the fall of prehistoric civilisations? That it's not a simple or straightforward discussion? The same pertains to the Roman Empire. Certainly, invasions by tribes from central and northern Europe played a role. The Empire was also experiencing a range of other problems. It was obliged to take up arms again. Indeed, at some point, one of the emperors, Diocletian, decided to divide the power of government among four individuals and create the Tetrarchy, and for a brief period Greece and the Balkan peninsula become a state within the overarching Roman state, with Thessaloniki as the capital of one half of the Roman Empire, and Galerius as leader. There is also one other truly critical change: a new religion crops up. One that is fundamentally different to anything the world had seen to that point.'

'Christianity?'

'Exactly! With the gradual expansion of this new religion, the world of antiquity as we know it begins to disappear. Former religions had a certain harshness to them, so what this new faith promised was truly inconceivable and unprecedented for the ancient world: complete equality for all – men, women, white, black, free, slaves, all are included. To be fair, perhaps it wasn't the very first time that something like this had been articulated, for ancient religions did promise something comparable but on a much smaller scale, or as part of mystical rituals like the Eleusinian Mysteries, which were addressed to those who were already initiated and who could travel to the city of Eleusis.'

'Why was the new religion able to spread like it did?'

'Perhaps because it did not wait for people to come it; it went to the people. After all, it was a religion that aimed to speak to everyone, from the wealthiest citizen to the poorest of poor slaves. The fact that now there were specific texts defining religious dogma also probably played a role, for the ancient world had not been able to rely on sacred texts. In any case, this new monotheistic faith spread throughout the entire empire, fully establishing itself despite the fact that its first few centuries of life were a tumult of internal disagreements and schisms that produced a range of different dogmas and heresies. This all occurred at a time when the Roman Empire was starting to tire and dwindle. At the beginning of the fourth century CE, Rome found itself in sore need of a makeover. One of its emperors, Constantine, decided that he, too, needed a change of scenery.

He had wearied of the same old same old: Colosseum, Palatine Hill, Tiber. Oof, enough already! He needed a holiday. A permanent one. So he took the entire capital with him all the way to an ancient Greek city, Byzantium, on the Bosphorus Strait.'

'Was that the name of the city? I thought the entire empire was called Byzantium.'

'You're getting it wrong. The word "Byzantine", used either to refer to the Empire or more generally as an adjective, is a neologism. In other words, something that we've coined more recently. People back then didn't refer to themselves or to their empire as Byzantine.'

'What did they call it?'

'Rome and the Roman Empire, of course! Because that's what it was. Or its extension, at least. It was relatively recently, in the sixteenth century, in fact, that we begin to call this period Byzantine because the new capital, Constantinople, was founded on the ancient city of Byzantium. It was named after its founder, a certain Byzas from the Doric colony of Megara in ancient Greece. Constantine, of course, changed the name to Constantinople, and it became the thousand-year-old capital of a new era as the sun began to set over the ancient world. The great schools of philosophy would padlock their doors, the Delphic oracle and the Panhellenic Olympic Games would come to an end, and the statues, whose obscene nudity embodied all that was wrong with an idolatrous faith, would be systematically destroyed.'

'What happened to all the knowledge accumulated during the ancient period?'

'Some discerning souls, aficionados of the pursuit of knowledge and the life of the mind, rescued as many texts as they could. Others were saved by virtue of their popularity. The least popular were lost. Sadly, too many! Some of the ancient temples were saved because they were converted to churches. In short, many years would pass before humans rediscovered their ancient legacy, and it happened bit by bit, step by painful step. For one, there were the Byzantine scholars and monks who almost blinded themselves in copying out the ancient texts they admired, and who, after the fall of the Byzantine Empire, packed their books and skedaddled over to Europe. There was also the fact that, by that time, Europeans, rubbing their eyes as they emerged from their Middle Ages, were fully primed to appreciate and be inspired by the ancient world. These developments are what led to the Renaissance. Let's take Bessarion from Trebizond in Pontic Greece, who contributed to this revival of letters, as an example. The beleaguered scholar and cleric fled to Italy, almost became pope twice – in fact, he would have, had he been Italian – and gifted his enormous collection of ancient Greek manuscripts to Venice. It still constitutes the core of the collections at the Biblioteca Marciana, or St. Mark's Library, one of the most important libraries in the world, which houses the oldest existing copy of the *Iliad*, the Venetus A.'

A SUDDEN THUD interrupted us. Then, after a slight judder, the elevator resumed its smooth descent. Startled, we lapsed into silence.

Once we had been let out, we thanked the firemen, and in a matter of minutes we were standing outside the building, relief written on our faces.

'Thanks so much for the company and the conversation. The time just flew by,' he said with an expression that I'm inclined to believe was fully earnest.

'No, thank *you*! I think I had more fun than you did.'

'Well, we managed to cover all of Greek antiquity in that elevator, didn't we? Pretty incredible!'

'Yes, true. It's almost like we planned it! As if someone knew exactly how much time was needed to fit all of antiquity in an elevator.'

We both laughed at the strange serendipity of it all.

Epilogue

ON THE PAVEMENT in front of the shopping centre, we both hung back.

'I hadn't realised how completely in the dark I was about antiquity. Also, that it's nowhere near as complex and boring as I thought it was. You covered so much information while we were in there, I'm afraid I won't remember even half of it.'

'Well, the truth is that I didn't cover the half of it – not even close. In any case, even though it's probably impossible to recap everything that we talked about in a few sentences, why don't you give it a try? I'm curious to see what you remember.'

'Alright then, here's my executive summary: the human presence on the planet began millions of years ago and for most of that time we lived like brutes, hunting and gathering food. That's the Palaeolithic period. We discovered fire, started to throw on some casual clothes, began to take care of each other as a community, and make art. At some point, boom, a big "revolution" occurs, and that's when we learn to cultivate the earth and raise animals, build houses and settle down in one place. That's the Neolithic period. In Greece, this lasted roughly from 7000 to 3000 BCE. How am I doing so far?'

'Great! Don't be too hard on yourself with all those dates ...'

'You know what, I feel like they help me understand the

breadth of this thing we call antiquity, and establish some order in my mind about what happened when. Around 3000 BCE is when the Bronze Age begins, with the first Cycladic culture and its beautiful figurines. Then came famous Minoan Crete with its dazzling palaces, and coming in last but not least is Mycenaean Greece, which provided many of the sources for later mythology. All this ended around 1100 BCE. Then, a bunch of civilisations fell and – ta da! – we're in the Dark Ages at around . . . 1200 BCE?'

He seemed a little stuck as he tried to remember. It was only to be expected.

'From 1050 BCE to 900 BCE.'

'Right! Because then came the Geometric Age and everyone bounced back. Greek colonies start dotting the coasts of the Mediterranean and the Black Sea, and right through to the Orientalising period at around . . . come on, help me out with the dates, won't you?'

'700 BCE.'

'Bingo! Yeah, so that's when the Greeks get a whiff of what is going on in the east, and they think, "Cool! We want some of that too!", and from 600 onwards we are in the Archaic period, which sets the stage for the development of basically everything that we understand as ancient Greek culture. Mainland Greece is now split into city-states, with Sparta at the top of the pile. The Greek colonies continue to spread throughout the Mediterranean, and the arts, branches of knowledge, philosophy, architecture, theatre, democracy, everything – they're all going gangbusters. Until the Persians pop up for the first war in 490 BCE and the second in 480 BCE. After its win in the Persian Wars, Greece enters the Classical period, and Athens is now all like, vogue, vogue, vogue and giving face and striking poses (sorry, I couldn't resist sneaking in one last nod to Madonna!). The arts, sciences, philosophy, rhetoric, they're growing like there's no tomorrow. In the middle of the Classical period, the Greeks get into a real humdinger of a civil war, the Peloponnesian War.'

'From 431 to 404 BCE, to be exact.'

'Yeah, I don't remember every little detail! But I do remember that with the exception of a short break, when Thebes rises to the top as the most powerful state, a kingdom in northern Greece – Macedonia – ends up taking the reins, as you like to say, at the end of the period. The Classical period ends with Alexander the Great, who charges over everything and literally changes the world map.'

'That's right! From 336 to 323 BCE.'

'Then comes the period of the Hellenistic Kingdoms, huge states that are constantly at each other's throats until a new superpower awakes in the Mediterranean. Rome proceeds to conquer the Greek states one by one and becomes ruler of all the Mediterranean in 30 BCE.'

'Actually, 31 BCE.'

'Yeah, but 30 is a round number, and I remember it.'

'But 31 was the year of the naval Battle of Actium. We can't get around that fact!'

'Alright, have it your way. Roman supremacy lasts until the capital is moved from Rome to Constantinople, and that's more or less the end of Greek antiquity. Oof, I did it!'

'When was the capital moved, though?'

'Even if you tell me, I'm sure I'll forget it.'

'324 CE.'

'You know, after all this, I feel like our conversation has given me more questions than answers.'

'That's only to be expected. It's not like we can cover all of the discipline in one brief conversation in an elevator. I hope you look for and find the answers to your new questions.'

'Yeah, that's the only thing I can guarantee. Now that things are a little clearer in my mind, I feel like I'll be better able to organise and remember each new bit of information. I am left with a certain feeling, though, a certain taste in my mouth – that despite the fact I grew up believing that the ancient Greek past was all glory, it really wasn't just that. I feel as if – oh, how can I put it? – as if we're doing it an injustice by describing it only as glorious. There are so many other sides to it.'

'Out of everything we discussed, what made the biggest impression in that respect?'

'Well, the influential role of other cultures and everything we took from them. But even though the ancient Greeks copied other cultures, they also took it in different directions and to different levels . . . then there's that awful civil war slap in the middle of one of the brightest periods in ancient Greek history; and the terrible tyrants and other types of rulers and leaders, all of whom were a little touched in the head, if we're being honest; as well as the fact that some of the figures we now most admire kind of went unnoticed in their own time. Oh, and we can't forget mythology's phallocentric perspective, the place of slaves in society, and the great advances in philosophy! It's really true that things are never all black or all white. You know what, though? I've had another realisation: everything you've just told me, it's just your version of events, isn't it?'

'Obviously. It stands to reason, doesn't it, that I would focus on what I find most interesting and important? But it's not just me, everyone does that. Do you think it's possible to approach the past without looking at it through the perspective of your own individual positionality? Aren't we all interested in and concerned with different issues? If you'd been in the elevator with a different archaeologist, they would have offered the same general outline but may well have focused on very different details. Given this opportunity to talk about antiquity through the lens of my discipline, I chose to focus on the human players that shaped it, in all their magical and complex idiosyncrasy. From the Minoan princess contemplating her impending journey to Egypt and priestess Carpathia's stubborn refusal to cultivate the land she'd been given, to the first winner of the first Olympic Games in history in 776 BCE, Coroebus of Elis, who was a cook.'

'But you didn't mention him!'

'There's a lot I didn't touch on. I did tell you, though, about Hippocleides, the high-spirited and twinkle-toed Athenian who pranced his way out of his marriage to Cleisthenes's daughter and the soon-to-be wife of Megacles, whose union produced the son who would go on to found democracy in Athens. There was also Phryne, the courtesan who fled her village and became the human representation of Aphrodite; and Corax, the rhetorician; Ageladas, the sculptor; Aeschylus, who was once a vineyard labourer; Euripides, who ended up being quite the misanthrope; and Simon the cobbler, who was the first to transcribe Socrates's dialogues. Despite all this, I must admit that there's a lot of information I just didn't have the time to mention. Did you really believe that it would be possible to fit all of antiquity in an elevator?'

'Well, I see that your preference is to tell the stories of particular individuals.'

'Yes, because as you heard, it's these small, strange stories about small, strange people that add up to this thing we call

History. I know that we are often dazzled by the big, important things: the great temples, the important museum exhibits, the enormous statues, the glittering gold wreaths, the large vases covered in decoration. Obviously, I'm not saying that they're not impressive, but we shouldn't overlook the smaller relics, which can also contain very rich and moving histories. For instance, tossed in a well in Athens's ancient Agora, numerous pieces of worthless vases were found. They lacked all decoration and had no artistic value whatsoever. Some of them, though, had etchings on them: one was a note someone had written to their neighbour: "When you return the tool I lent you, leave it under the threshold because I'm gone." Another is essentially the oldest surviving booty call. A young man, Arkesimos, left a note telling his lover, Eumelis, to come meet him. Clearly impatient and keyed up, it looks like he glanced at the note before leaving it and found it lacking in urgency, so among the other lines of text, he squeezed in the phrase *os tachos* – in other words, "make it snappy"!'

'Hahaha! He wanted her bad. And did she go?'

'We don't know.'

'What a pity! You know, we didn't get to talk about their love lives and what they thought about sex.'

'That's a big topic if ever there was one!'

'You know what strikes me as strange? What's the deal with sexuality in ancient Greece? What did being "straight" or "gay" mean back then?'

'I'll answer that by pointing to some examples from ancient religion and mythology. Zeus, as we all know, was the biggest Lothario ever. Besides the countless young women he seduced, he also found time to woo young men, the most famous of whom was Ganymede. Apollo had flings galore with both women and men. Callisto was a nymph and follower of Artemis who was seduced by Zeus in the form of Artemis, and you know what? It was all A-OK with Callisto. Heracles also fell in love often, with both women and his comrades in arms.'

'What are you saying? That they were all bisexual?'

'Why insist on pigeonholing them in terms of current understandings of sex, eroticism, and gendered identity? Don't forget that we live in a society that has been shaped as much by the lingering traces of the Puritanism and conservatism of the Middle Ages as by the rigid moralism of the monotheistic religions that now reign supreme over the planet. Sexuality in the ancient world was neither strictly binary nor singular. In fact, heterosexuality was not patrolled and protected by all the prohibitions and guilt complexes that we have today. Remember that perceptions of sexuality have really changed over the centuries.'

'I'm just struck by the fact that they had gods with such a – how shall I put it? – *range* of sexual appetites. I mean, they worshipped them, they were part of the religion, so that means that their behaviours were accepted, perhaps even seen as normal. In any case, you've got me thinking . . . I suppose this is yet another thing that knowledge of the past can teach us. But there is one thing, mate, that the past *doesn't* and *can't* teach us. Do you know what it is?' His expression was mischievous. 'What do women really want?'

'Ha! I've got you covered on this one too. They want exactly what men want. What every human being wants: security.'

'Security from what?'

'From anything that we fear. And what is it that strikes terror into the depths of the human heart the world over? Death. Once again, archaeology comes to the rescue, because it helps us understand time, space, humanity. We seem to believe that if and when we finally understand time, when we can wrap our minds around it, we'll be able to cut it down to our size; we'll be able to handle it, and therefore outrun it.'

'No matter what we talk about, you always return to human psychology.'

'I told you from the very beginning – archaeology, the knowledge and discovery of our past, serves as a playground in which the human imagination, perception, and psyche can run free. All our experiences, all our anxieties and joys, spring from our past. The true wonder of archaeology lies in the fact that it can serve as a collective form of psychoanalysis for the entire human race.'

'OK, one final question as a parting shot: what do you personally find to be the greatest insight gained from your knowledge of the past?'

'What do I personally find most important? The hetairai, the prostitutes, the slaves, the persecuted, the oddballs, the misfits, all the square pegs who were condemned for not fitting into the round holes of their society. Also, the fact that all the great advances we've made as humans were catalysed by these very same oddballs, outcasts, dissidents; the pariahs in society. Knowledge of our past tells us, once and for all, that humans have always persevered in the face of adversity, that we have grown and moved forward through the turmoil and reversals of change. Human culture is one of constant change, perpetual motion. Classical Athens executed Socrates, one of its few home-grown philosophers who hadn't migrated there from other parts of the Greek world. Perhaps the most seminal philosopher in the history of human thought. It's analogous to what had happened a few years earlier, when the prevailing pieties of the period had led to Anaxagoras's exile for his attempts to vanquish superstition, or to the way in which Alcidamas had been ignored and spurned.'

'Hey, this is the first time you're referring to this Alcidamas fellow!'

'I know. There were many important figures and events I didn't talk about, for the simple reason that I didn't have the time. Alcidamas, my friend, was a philosopher who dared to condemn the evils of slavery. He declared that all people are born equal and the same, that no one is predestined to either freedom or slavery, and that therefore these categories are human inventions fundamentally at odds with the truth of our nature.'

'You mean that way back in the ancient world we already find people making arguments for the equality of all human beings? That's wild!'

'Not everyone was making this argument. Aristotle, for example, despite being a philosopher with a capital "P", did not agree. He found the idea that some people were destined to be the property of others completely reasonable. You see: two radically opposing viewpoints produced in tandem. The same heady cultural brew that nurtured Alcimadas and the other philosophers who identified liberty and self-determination as general human values, also produced the Aristotles who impeded the realisation of these values.'

'Shame on Aristotle! On the other hand, you know what I'm thinking? No matter how great a philosopher he was, he obviously had his blind spots.'

'Don't we all? This is why I'm telling you that it is both limiting and unjust to see the human past as either unadulterated good or bad. Instead, we need to examine the nuances of their coexistence. Classical Athens was very much on the cutting edge in some things, while at the same time paralysed by fear in others. Obviously, dissension is never easily tolerated by the status quo, and when dissidents are too loud and persistent, they are marginalised as pariahs. But even in a world with only a handful of such audacious and reflective individuals, it is neither the mainstream nor the apathetic or compromising majorities that prevail – this has been true through time immemorial. The world we live in belongs to the children and the grandchildren of the audacious thinkers, and in particular to those who choose to follow in the footsteps of their pariah ancestors. The world has never belonged to the children who blindly accept what is handed down to them by their parents, but to the ones who believe in the persecuted, who are thorns in the sides of complacency. Because it is only through dissent and disobedience that we blaze new paths forward, paths and avenues that will only be valued in hindsight, for they tend to be overlooked in their own time. History is full of pioneers who were spurned by their contemporaries: Anaxarchus and Pyrrho, for example, part of Alexander the Great's entourage to Asia. Pyrrho was fascinated by the Persian magicians and Indian Buddhists he encountered, and on his return to Greece he founded the school of Scepticism. Anaxarchus, on the other hand, was perhaps the only one who dared be brutally honest with Alex.'

'Why? What did he say?'

'When Alexander the Great declared himself a deity as the son of Zeus-Ammon, Anaxarchus pointed to one of the wounds on the self-anointed god's body and said that it looked like it was bleeding mortal blood. When the doctor recommended a poultice, Anaxarchus muttered: "Excellent, our 'god' is pinning his hopes on a poultice!" According to legend, he also made Alexander cry when he told him that in all likelihood there were countless other worlds as yet unknown to humans, and that Alex hadn't even conquered the entirety of the only one familiar to them!'

'That sounds to me like quantum physics and parallel universes.'

'Yes, it's wonderful how boundless and timeless the human intellect and imagination are! What's even more wonderful is that today they can meaningfully contribute to formal disciplines of study and thereby grow new forms of knowledge. Did you know that even the word "galaxy" has an ancient Greek origin?'

'What do you mean?'

'Heracles's extraordinary strength derived from the fact that he was nursed by the queen of the gods, Hera. You see, after he was born, Zeus got Hermes to put the infant to nurse at the sleeping Hera's breast, even though she wanted nothing to do with her husband's child by another woman. At one point, though, Hera wakes up, and, startled, she shoves the infant away from her. The drops of her milk that fall to earth turn into white lilies, and the milk that spatters all over the heavens creates the Galaxy. This is why in English we call it the Milky Way!'

'Wow! Poor Heracles – he too seems to have been hounded since birth.'

'Yet despite it all, he persevered and succeeded. Like so many mortals who were hounded by their societies. Like Hipparchia of Maroneia! I can't believe I didn't remember to talk about her until now. A real force to be reckoned with, I tell you!'

'Why? What did she do?'

'Her parents moved from Maroneia in Thrace to Athens. That's where Hipparchia met a rather eccentric philosopher called Crates.'

'What do you mean by eccentric?'

'Non-conformist, my friend. He was a cynic philosopher who renounced all material goods. He had been born into a very wealthy family in Thebes, but he left it all behind him, gifted his property to the city, and left for Athens. That's where Hipparchia fell madly in love with him for his mind. Her parents were dead set against the union. They even begged Crates to convince their daughter to let him go. According to legend, Crates threw off his clothes and, standing completely naked in front of her, he said: "This is my only property!" This only made Hipparchia even madder about him. They lived a happy life together by the looks of things, outside the bounds of social convention, even though they were denounced by many. Back then, you see, society could not accept a couple who respected each other and lived their lives in full equality. There's a story that at some point Hipparchia got into a dispute with another philosopher, Theodorus the Atheist. Angered and wishing to shame her, he pulled off her garment and left her there naked. Hipparchia, however, couldn't have cared less.'

'She had no issue with her naked body?'

'Well, she had no truck with body shaming, that's for sure. She was beyond such pettiness. Theodorus, even angrier now, turned and said, "Who is the woman who has turned her back on spinning and weaving?" She replied, "Do I appear to you to have made the wrong decision, if instead of wasting my time at the loom, I devote it to philosophy?" Oh yes, she gave as good as she got! Back then, she was merely a colourful character; now, however, we see how truly extraordinary she was. This, of course, is a form of divine justice if you think about it: out-casts and dissidents who are hounded and tormented by one generation are then revered by the next. Somewhere out there, wherever that may be, the souls of Socrates and all those who followed in his subversive footsteps can hopefully find some peace in this knowledge. Because in the end it was the children of convention, of orthodoxy, who went on to praise and cele-brate the pariahs' achievements. Besides, the world belongs to the children. Heraclitus said it himself.'

'The "obscure" philosopher? Heraclitus who spouted some nonsense about Homer and said that he ought to be thrashed?'

'That's him. He spent his final years in seclusion and died alone, out of sight of the adults he spurned, and who in turn spurned him. He spoke only to the young children who came to play in the courtyard of the Temple of Artemis in Ephesus. In that temple is where he left the only book he ever wrote. Per-sonally, I like to think that this book of Heraclitus's contained more truth about everything than any other book in the history of mankind. Unfortunately, all we have left of his book is a few sentences. One of them says: "Time is a child at play. The king-dom of this world belongs to a child."'

He thanked me, we exchanged telephone numbers and social media handles, and bid each other goodbye. As he turned the corner, I realised that I had not asked him what he did for a living. Had I monopolised the conversation? A tiny spark of guilt flared for only a split second, because then I turned, saw a taxi approaching in the distance, and flagged it down.

I climbed in and asked the driver to take me to the Archae-ological Museum.

In a couple of minutes, we were at a complete standstill, cars on all sides. The drivers had even stopped honking, for the line of traffic as far as the eye could see clearly communicated the inevitability of delay. For a few minutes, the only thing that could be heard was the music pouring from the radio.

'It must be another demonstration,' the driver said nonchalantly.

'Doesn't matter.'

'It looks like we'll be here a while.'

'I'm not in a hurry.'

'Why are you going to the museum? Are you visiting from out of town?'

'No, I'm an archaeologist.'

'Ah, archaeology! Bravo! You must know all about our glorious history and the wisdom of our ancestors. It's sad how far we've fallen!'

'Well, I wouldn't say they were all wise. They were just regular people.'

'What do you mean? There's Leonidas, Achilles, Aristotle . . . they were all great heroes, weren't they? And what about all those other important ancient figures? Admittedly, I didn't really learn it all that well at school, so I may be getting some things mixed up, but . . .'

'It's not all that hard to get to know the past.'

'Easy for you to say. You studied it. For the rest of us, it's a complete mystery!'

'I can tell you about it, if you'd like, and in simple language to boot. We have plenty of time . . .'

αἰὼν παῖς ἐστι παίζων πεσσεύων·
παιδὸς ἡ βασιληίη.

Time is a child at play
The kingdom of this world belongs to a child.

TIMELINE

3.5 MILLION YEARS

Palaeolithic Age: Humans emerge in the natural world, rise on their two feet, create tools, and discover fire. The journey begins!

Mesolithic Age: Times are changing. →

7,000 BCE

NEOLITHIC AGE: HUMANS BEGIN TO PLANT CROPS, SHEAR AND MILK THEIR LIVESTOCK, BUILD HOMES.

3,000 BCE

Cycladic Culture: Marble, sea salt, sun, and figurines. →

MINOAN CULTURE: PALACES, WEALTH, AND OPULENCE. OH, AND LINEAR A.

↓

Mycenaean Culture: War, more palaces, and the wellspring of myth. Oh, and Linear B.

↓

1,050 BCE **The Dark Ages: Trials, tribulations, and recovery.**

900 BCE

Geometric Period: The beginning of the historic period. More new and improved writing. Development.

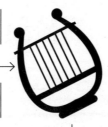

700 BCE

Archaic Period: Arts, philosophy, theatre. In a nutshell, culture shines bright.

490–480 BCE

The Persian Wars, or the bullies get their comeuppance.

CLASSICAL PERIOD: THE ZENITH OF CULTURE AND THE GREATEST CIVIL WAR.

336–323 BCE

As a lark, Alexander the Great builds an empire.

Hellenistic Period: Numerous kingdoms result in numerous conflicts.

ROME, CONQUEROR OF THE WORLD, FALLS IN LOVE WITH GREECE.

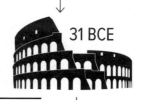

31 BCE

With the founding of Constantinople, the ancient world comes to an end.

324 CE